Counting Down T[...]

and other love stories

for Girls Who Like Girls

from

Freya Publications

and

When Sally Met Sally

Visit Freya Publications

at

www.freyapublications.com

Visit When Sally met Sally

at

www.whensallymetsally.co.uk

Copyright Freya Publications and When Sally Met Sally 2013
All rights reserved. No part of this book may be reproduced or transmitted in any form by any means electrical or mechanical, including photocopy without permission in writing from the publisher.

Unless otherwise stated, all characters within this work are fictitious. Any resemblance to real persons living or dead is purely coincidental.

Produced in the United Kingdom for Freya Publications and When Sally Met Sally

Counting Down the Seconds

ISBN 978-1-291-45318-8

First Published 1st June 2013

by Freya Publications and When Sally Met Sally

FOREWORD

When Sally Met Sally and Freya Publications are proud to present 'Counting Down The Seconds', a collection of fifteen short stories for women who love women.

We announced a writing competition in January 2013, asking female writers of LGBT fiction to send us their stories. There were no strict rules: we merely asked for stories that touched on some aspect of attraction, romance, relationships and/or love (requited or unrequited) between women.

Encouraging people to set their imaginations free and to write in whatever genre they enjoyed the most, we were delighted with the diverse range of stories we received—from science fiction to period drama, from sex comedies to darker tales of woe, from literary fiction to "chick lit", from stories set in fantasy worlds to more "down to earth" settings.

The fifteen stories in this anthology are those that received the highest scores from the four competition judges (two representatives from When Sally Met Sally and Freya Publications, and two independent lesbian fiction critics).

The overall winner of the competition was Lexy Wealleans for her romantic love story set in the far future, 'Counting Down The Seconds'. Congratulations, Alex!

But our heartfelt congratulations go also to the other fourteen talented writers whose amazingly diverse stories we are proud to publish in this anthology.

It's important to note that the order of stories in this anthology is completely random, and is in no way a reflection of the ranking of the stories by the judges.

We hope you enjoy our collection.

About the publishers

Freya Publications is a specialist publisher of women's writing and lesbian fiction. Check out Freya's website here: http://www.freyapublications.com

When Sally Met Sally is an online magazine for gay/bisexual women with a focus on culture, entertainment, lifestyle, same-sex parenting and relationships: http://www.whensallymetsally.co.uk/

Acknowledgments

Many thanks to Terry Baker and Jo Wrench for helping us judge the competition, and kindly taking the time to read though all the stories received.

Thanks also to Sam Lane for his wonderful work designing the front cover. More great examples of Sam's work can be viewed on his website: cargocollective.com/samlane

CONTENTS

COUNTING DOWN THE SECONDS by LEXY WEALLEANS- 9

CONSUMED by CHRIS MCMURRAY - 27

A PHILADELPHIA STORY by MELODY BREYER-GRELL -65

11:55 by DENISE WARNER-GREGORY - 87

SHINJUKU NIGHTSHIFT by JADE DU PREEZ - 97

THE AFFAIR by MELANIE KING - 108

IT COMES NATURALLY by RUTH MOORMAN - 128

LEARNING TO LOVE SPIDERS by SASHA FAULKS - 148

ROLLER COASTER OF WAITING by OLGA GUYMON - 158

MORGAN LE FEY by JOSIE TERESI - 174

THE MISSING PIECE by DANNI PEARSON - 191

SECRETS OF THE HEART by LIZ KERR - 216

INHERITANCE by HELEN LARDER - 241

SATIN OVER SAND by SAM PATERSON-SLEEP- 259

A SIMPLE GESTURE by EFFI MAI- 270

COUNTING DOWN THE SECONDS

by

Lexy Wealleans

Lexy Wealleans is a scientist and writer. She spends most of her working day struggling with spreadsheets, and wishing she lived in an Enid Blyton novel instead. Counting Down the Seconds is her first piece of published fiction for adults.

16 years, 3 months and 8 days

I have my clock fitted the weekend I turn sixteen. It sits flush against the skin of my wrist, fuelled by my heartbeat, counting down the seconds to destiny. On the way home, I trace the outline of it, the skin red and sensitive. It hurts, dully, throbbing with my every pulse, like a toothache.

The clocks are new, trendy. They were only released last year, and within weeks they'd been seen on the wrists of the rich and famous. It was best, though, to have them fitted young. The papers were full of people who had paid for a clock, only to find their timer already zeroed, and their chance at meeting their soulmate gone forever.

The next day at school, my friends crowd round, checking their dates against mine.

"God, Imogen," they say. "You're going to be totally old by the time you zero." That's the phrase now—to zero. It's a clinical phrase for a moment that, by all accounts, is anything but.

Julia is the last of the crowd to leave for lessons. I've always liked her, always noticed when we stood next to each other in the lunch queue, when my arm would press against the side of her breast. She ducks her head to catch my eye and smiles, ruefully.

"Not us, then." She shakes her head.

"Only five years for me."

I'm less disappointed than I thought I might be. Instead, I take to imagining the moment I zero. I imagine the weather, all blue skies and heat. I imagine the things I'll say and how she'll laugh and smile.

My dream world carries me along from day to day, and the clock on my wrist buffers me from heartbreak.

*

13 years, 10 months and 20 days

My eighteenth birthday comes and goes, and university calls. I throw myself into the life—the work, the parties, the sex. I sleep with the clockless, and other slow-burners like me. There's no need for commitment—the countdown embedded in my wrist is a better deterrent than a wedding ring ever could be.

One night, the hall bar runs a "speed meeting" night. Like speed dating, but with no romantic intent. Or at least, it's not supposed to have any romantic intent. The bell's just rung and a new partner moves to sit in front of me, when from somewhere in the room comes the distinctive beeping of two clocks zeroing together.

The girl opposite follows my gaze.

"You clocked?" she says. I hold up my wrist, pulling the cuff back.

"I've got years left." She does the same, just enough to reveal the edge of the number display. The line of digits is long, but not as long as mine.

"Me too. Still, that means we get to have plenty of fun in the meantime though, right?" She winks, and runs a hand through short hair.

I don't go back to my own room that night, or the night after. It's easy, comfortable, with Jen. It tends to be, when there's no expectations, when both of you know you're only a stop-gap girlfriend.

*

12 years, 2 months and 13 days

It is just an ordinary day, an ordinary lecture. I'm late, which is also entirely usual.

Jen sits at the back, paying no attention at all, texting under the desk. There's no seats near her, and I have to slip into the closest empty seat.

"Sorry," I whisper, too loudly, to the girl next to me. She turns to me, shifting sideways on her seat. I've never really believed those stories, you know, where noise fades and your world narrows to just one person. I want to say that in that moment I understand, that she turns in slow motion, the light catching her hair and our eyes lock in sudden and inevitable understanding.

It's not like that at all. She rolls her eyes, and turns straight back to the lecture, her pen barely breaking stride as she takes notes. My stomach is not so easily settled, twisting and churning with the sickening pull of attraction.

I'm afraid I don't pay much attention to the lecture—the finer points of drug quality assurance go quite over my head. Instead I'm watching her as she pays attention. Her pen moves across the paper, writing notes in handwriting so small I can barely read it. Only when the lecturer calls the half-time break does she turn back to me, the side of her mouth slightly upturned, and I know I've been caught staring.

"I'm Imogen," I say, plastering on what I hope is my most charming smile.

"Kate." Her smile is tight, fixed. "Excuse me." She slides past, down the stairs and out of the theatre. Jen calls to me from the back of the room, shifting and making space for me to join her. I pay just as much attention after the break as I had before, my eyes fixed to the back of a head of golden hair, my thoughts drifting pleasantly.

*

10 years, 6 months and 7 days

"Come on, Jen," I whine, "we'll miss the start of the match." She's dragging along behind me, holding doors open for the world and his wife.

"Oh, there's no hurry. You know England's gonna smash Tonga to bits. We won't miss anything."

I wait, impatiently, barely stopping my foot from tapping. Finally, when no one else seems to be approaching, Jen finally lets the door swing shut, and follows me down the steps towards the students' union bar.

There's a girl coming up the other way, and we dance awkwardly from side to side. Finally, we manage to move past each other, but as we do she trips, and her bag tumbles from her shoulder, books and notes flying down the steps.

Jen bends down, stopping to help the girl pick up her files. I see it almost in slow motion, as they reach for the same piece of paper. They pause, eyes locked together, hands touching. Jen laughs, shakily, her breath coming in machine-gun bursts of nervousness.

I wait, but neither of them seem to plan on speaking any time soon.

"This is Jen," I volunteer. "Jen, this is…"

"Jenna. I'm Jenna." Oh god. Not only are they wearing matching lovesick grins, but they have matching names.

We sit at the sticky tables, the three of us. I'm the only one watching the rugby. I knew it was coming, of course—I couldn't miss the soft tick of her clock as we made love, couldn't miss the date circled in her diary, or the way I'd catch her hunched over her wrist in the early morning hours, watching the seconds slip away.

At half time I stand up, the chair legs scraping sharply across the floor.

"Do you want another drink?" Neither Jen or her new girl answer, and I go to the bar alone.

There's no shame in being dropped so unceremoniously, I tell myself. Not when soul mates are involved. Yet as I stand waiting for my drink, I look down at my still counting clock and, for the first time, feel the faintest stirrings of regret.

England lose to Tonga, 57 to 12.

*

10 years, 5 months and 21 days

The campus is knee-deep in unexpected snow. It's also deserted, only the foolish and the desperately keen bothering to wade across to lectures. I'm not sure which camp I fall into—probably both. After all, there's only one reason I hauled myself out of bed and into freezing temperatures, and as I turn a corner, I see that reason picking her way towards me.

I smile and wave, watching her cautious progress. She's bundled up adorably, with a thick red scarf and a knitted hat pulled right down over her ears. My heart flips, one-two, and the feeling is lustfully echoed in other parts of my anatomy.

I'm not watching where I'm walking, and tread on a pebble buried under the snow. The soles of my boots slide on the ice. I wobble, arms windmilling to keep my balance, but my ankle gives way and buckles sideways. My feet slip out from under me, and I go down with a thud. The wind's knocked out of me, and I lay on my back in the snow, panting. I hear footsteps crunching closer, and then Kate's there, hovering above me. She crouches down, one hand resting on her knee, the other readjusting her scarf tighter around her neck.

"Are you alright?" I have to look away, hiding the lump in my throat and the pulse beating wildly under my skin. There's something in her tone that makes me think that she's not asking about my ankle. "Think you can walk?"

I nod, embarrassed, and she holds her hand out to pull me up. Our feet slide together on the ice, and she clings to my coat for support. Our breaths merge together in the cold air, cloudy trails spiralling up and away.

Once we're steady again, we pick our way across the frozen ground, treading carefully. When we get there, there's no one else in the lecture theatre, not even the lecturer. We settle into the benches together, coats laid out to dry behind us.

"Guess we're just too keen," I mutter, embarrassed. She laughs, and leans back against the hard wooden seat, stretching her legs out into the aisle. "Dunno why we bothered today."

"This is my favourite lecture," she says. "It'd take a lot more than snow to put me off."

"Really?" It's hard to believe: clinical biochemistry is no one's favourite subject. "Why?"

She blushes, and stares into the middle distance, clearly weighing her words carefully.

"Because," she starts, "it's the one I share with you."

I pull her in, and kiss her. And immediately wonder why we haven't been doing this all along, because if there's anything in the world better than kissing Kate, I don't know what it is. As we pull apart I press my fingers to my lips, trying to recover some of my bravado. Her hands are still fisted in the material of my jumper, and she looks as flustered as I feel.

*

9 years, 3 months and 29 days

"Trafalgar Square? Really?" Kate sits up in bed, and her movement forces me up too. The duvet slips down across her bare shoulders, and I follow its path lightly with my fingertips.

"What's wrong with waiting to zero in Trafalgar square?" I'm crosser than my tone indicates, not wanting to be mocked.

"Nothing, babe. Nothing." She pushes wisps of hair from my face. "It's just—isn't it a bit clichéd?"

"Well, perhaps I'll be there," she says, "right in front of you as you zero."

"I don't think it works like that. I've already met you."

"I know, Immy." She pulls me back, bringing my head down to rest on her shoulder, rubbing her nails in circles across my scalp. "But perhaps, if you want it, you can change your fate."

*

8 years, 1 month and 15 days

"Did you hear," Kate says one day, quite out of the blue, "about that woman whose clock stopped the day she gave birth?"

I lean on my spade, stopping for a moment to admire my work. The rose, a belated birthday gift from Kate, sits firmly in the earth against the fence under the shade of the apple tree.

"Well? Did you?"

I heard. Clocks are less newsworthy, these days. They're a bit old hat, really, and only make the front pages when something weird happens, or something goes wrong. Like the woman and the baby, or other, less happy, stories. There was one, a few months back, where a man found his clock mysteriously frozen, stuck at 18 months. He'd tapped it, and shaken it, even wondered if a battery had gone. It wasn't a faulty battery, the clock manufacturer said, but a car crash a thousand miles away.

I keep my own clock hidden under wide watch straps and chunky bracelets and try to ignore the constant countdown.

*

7 years, 2 months and 2 days

The hospital corridor is cold, the chair they give me hard and uncomfortable. I shift, rolling my shoulders, feeling as the bones click together in my neck.

The clock on my wrist keeps ticking, but I love my daughter anyway.

*

4 years, 2 months and 2 days

"I can't do this anymore," Kate says. Her voice is quite low, calm and collected. Her face, too, is expressionless as she watches Ellie pull the wrapping off her presents.

"What?"

"Mummy, look!" Ellie efficiently cuts us off, waving a new doll excitedly. I force a smile for my daughter, pulling her up onto my lap and burying my face in her hair.

The afternoon passes quickly, as they always do, and before I have a chance to stop and think I find myself ready for bed. I sit perched on the edge, staring down at my feet as Kate rustles behind me, getting ready to sleep.

"Have you met someone else?" The words are large in my throat, sticking to the roof of my mouth. I don't turn around, but I hear her shake her head.

"No, but you will." There's little arguing with the logic. My watch covers the clock, but it doesn't remove the fact that I'm still counting down. I peel off the strap, watching the numbers tick over. There's still more than four years to go. "Ellie and I need someone who's not going to run off and leave us."

"I won't," I say, "soul mates aren't always a romantic thing. You said yourself, about the woman and her baby."

"But I know you, remember. Trafalgar Square, Imogen, is not a platonic gesture."

It's the kind of answer that isn't really an answer, and it's the only answer I'm likely to get.

The lights go out with a click, sending us into darkness. As I slide under the cold covers, I feel her warmth come creeping towards me through the mattress. She's close enough to touch, close enough to roll over and hold, to bury my face in her hair as I have done almost every evening for six years.

My hands stay by my side, the gap between us unbreached.

*

2 months and 2 days

"Happy birthday, miss mouse," I say. The garden is decked with bunting and balloons, full of Ellie's excited school friends. The plants, now, are well established; my rose twines right up through the apple tree, too fixed in place to ever move.

My daughter squints up at me, creasing her eyes against the sunlight.

"I'm not a mouse," she says.

"No? Then who are you?"

"I'm Ellie, of course." Then she's gone, running down the lawn to the knot of children, poking at a bucket of water and flower petals with a stick. I stand and watch them from the patio for a while, until a shadow moves down the kitchen steps behind me.

"Glad you could make it," Kate says. "Nice to have some adult company for a change." I can hear the smile in her words, even if I can't see it.

"Where's Alice?" I can't quite keep the bitterness from my voice, and I hate myself for it. Kate comes to stand beside me, shoulders almost touching. She shakes her head, hand rubbing self-consciously at her wrist, scratching through her sleeve.

"Right now? I don't know," she says. "Could be anywhere at all." She seems to catch herself, glancing down at her hands, stopping the scratching and crossing them in front of herself defensively.

"I'm sorry to hear that."

"No you're not, Immy." She's right. I nod, not speaking. I don't trust my voice to stay calm and steady, and I really don't want to cause a scene. Not in front of Ellie, not in front of her friends and their parents. My hand's reaching for the garden gate, resting on the latch, ready to leave.

"You must be almost zeroed these days." Her words check my footsteps, but I don't turn round. I stop, inches from the stained wood.

"That's really none of your business anymore, is it?" Then the gate is open, and I'm out on the gravel driveway, crunching towards my car. Her words are faint, and I have to strain to hear them.

"Good luck."

*

4 hours

"You're really not going to go?" Jen's voice down the phone line is tinny.

"No, I'm really not."

"But you've had this planned, the whole time I've known you." I shrug, even though she can't see me.

"I'm done with dreaming, Jen. And I'm done with the clock." I swallow, and close my eyes. "It cost me you. It cost me Julia, and… Kate." My throat closes around my words, and Jen is silent until I can breathe again. "I want to decide for myself, this time."

I put the phone down on the desk. The computer's gone to the screensaver and I watch the photos of Ellie flicker past. I try to imagine, without the years of romanticised planning, how my zeroing will go. I list every person in the building. I suppose there might be visitors, corporate guests, but sat in my office I'm hardly likely to meet them.

What would happen, I wonder, if I locked myself in? If, when my numbers finally stilled, I was sat alone, staring at the computer screen. Would that mean the internet was my soulmate, or just that I'd missed my opportunity?

I remember Kate's words, from half a lifetime ago. Perhaps, if you really want, you can change your fate.

I stand up, pulling my coat from the hook on the back of the door. I call for a taxi as I rush down the stairs, two at a time, and stand fidgeting in the High Street until it comes.

"Where to, love?" says the cabbie.

In movies or books they'd have something clever to say, something pre-prepared and romantic.

"The station, please. And I'm late."

The cab accelerates away, and I'm still not sure it's the right thing to do.

*

10 minutes

The escalators are full at Charing Cross, and so I take the stairs, dodging the crowds that pour in the opposite direction. It's hot on the platform, close and stifling. The collar of my work shirt sticks close to my neck, and I have to peel the material away from my skin.

I'm starting to feel a little nervous. No one wants to meet their soulmate pressed sweatily between strangers on the underground.

I check my wrist. I've got time. The pillar by the ticket machines is mirrored, and I stand in front of it, ignoring the press of people moving around me. I push the hair back from my face, straighten out the creases in my shirt front, make sure my necklace is the right way round. As I raise my hands to my neck, the ring on my finger flashes gold. I consider taking it off. After all, I'm no longer technically supposed to be wearing it.

It's tight around my finger, unmoving. I pull uselessly for a moment, then give up. My soulmate, I think, will understand.

*

3 minutes

The sky is as blue as I ever dreamed it could be, the air as warm. In all my imaginings, I couldn't have wished for a more perfect day than I've been given.

The square is heaving with tourists, all kitted with cameras. As I cross the road, hurrying between taxis, I scan the faces of the crowd. I look for anyone checking their wrist, or scanning for my face in return.

*

1 minute

There are boot-covered feet in front of my face. Legs lead up and away, and I turn my head to trace their lines. Over a slim waist, a tattersall shirt, and up into a face I already know. Her shape is outlined in the sunlight, her hair a halo around her head. My heart flutters tightly in my chest, and I remember this feeling.

"I couldn't not be here," Kate says, "not when…"

She holds out her hand to pull me up, and I clasp her wrist, her pulse beating slow and strong under my hand. Against her skin a newly-fitted clock counts down the seconds, in perfect time with my own.

Zero.

CONSUMED

by

Chris McMurray

Chris McMurray currently lives in Belfast, Northern Ireland, after living and working in the United States for a number of years. The inspiration for this short story was taken from her life in the USA.

Chris has been seriously committed to writing since she was twelve years old. In her later teens, she started using the freedom of the pen to really express her love for women.

She has been submitting short stories and poems to various sites on the Web, with the hopes that those who read them will share them with the women they love.

Chris's life is now shared blissfully with her partner Anne.

PART ONE

It was the summer of my twenty-seventh year and I was struggling with the development of my fourth novel. I had hit a brick wall with the creation of the book's characters, and I had spent endless days writing page after page of worthless text, only to wad them up and toss them in the trash, which was now overflowing with debris of dead characters. The walls of my studio home were closing in around me, making my writer's block even more dangerous. I knew I had a talent and had successfully published my first three novels in less than two years, but now my agent and publisher were both pressuring me to meet an upcoming deadline for a first draft.

Before becoming a published author, my words used to spring from my head to my computer screen with relative ease and it was such a joyful part of my life to tell the stories that grew endlessly in my imagination. Now with deadlines, book signings and public relations activities, I felt pressured to write, to produce a certain number of pages that felt more like a chore than a joy.

It was then that I decided to break away. I asked a friend to house-sit while I packed my bags and my laptop and drove north. The Smokey Mountains of western North Carolina have always seemed a second home for me—a place of peace and relaxation, worlds apart from the hustle and bustle of the city. It was there in the deep woods that I felt I could find the flow of words that had eluded me and finally finish the draft that my agent was due in three months.

I would escape to the woods where I had spent my summers as a child and later as a college student. I was fortunate to still have family connections in the general area of Asheville and a cousin around my age had hooked me up with my old summer job. Southwest of Asheville by several hours there was a vacancy for a fire watcher: someone who could spend endless hours in a fire tower watching for signs of a forest fire. It was here that I had first begun writing during those endless summer hours, as a way to pass the time between shifts at the fire tower.

Each tower was generally staffed with two persons who would work eight-hour shifts each before being relieved by the oncoming shift. It was far from strenuous work—the most laborious task was climbing the two hundred and four metal steps to reach the top of the observation tower. There were usually two or more high-powered telescopes positioned in the observation post that could be pivoted around to cover the entire scope of the assigned area. Even with the naked eye you could see for miles in every direction, and after the morning mist burned off, the sun would illuminate a sea of evergreens.

The local weather station was forecasting a dry summer, so the risk of forest fire would be elevated. Careless campers in the area would at times lose control of campfires, or a cigarette butt would be tossed out of a window, and on the rare occasion of a summer thunderstorm, a lightning strike could cause the forest to go up like sticks in a tinderbox. So, even though I would need to remain vigilant for signs of fire, there would be plenty of time to spend writing.

I would be sharing a cabin with Morgan Montgomery, a college senior who had spent several summers on the fire watch. Morgan was a major in Forestry Sciences and would work the late daylight hours, which had the greatest potential of fires, while I would be responsible for the early morning shift. I wasn't in need of the money: my novels had done well and I could just have easily rented or bought a cabin in the woods to do nothing but focus on writing, but the lure of adventure and recapturing a little of my youth spurred me to accept this position.

My Land Rover easily climbed the foothills and wound around the tight curves as I drove through the mountains to Franklin. I was surrounded by green as I drove through valleys and dense forest, an occasional waterfall springing to life in my window as I drove. When I finally pulled up to the cabin, it was nearly three in the afternoon and the shadows were cooling down for the evening as I unloaded my bags and walked inside.

The cabin was not lushly decorated or furnished with the amenities of today's comfort, but I immediately felt at home with the rustic wooden beams and oversized furniture. I was pleased to see a swing on the front porch which displayed a panoramic view of a lush valley pasture. Standing there, I could look across and see the hillside and valley, dotted with black cattle grazing on the rich, tall grasses. The air bathed my lungs with its pureness, the scent of evergreen cleansing the exhaust smoke from my body with every breath.

I located a bedroom that appeared to be vacant and was busy hanging my clothes and emptying my bags into the dresser when I heard the front door open. When I looked out from the closet, a young brunette was standing in the doorway.

"I thought I heard someone pull up," she said with a grin. "I am Morgan. You must be Jordan. I have read all of your books and I must say you have a terrific talent." She stepped inside the room. "I nearly fainted when I was told that you would be my partner this summer."

"Well thank you, Morgan," I said rather blandly. "I had this job when I was in college as well and it is where I first began writing. I have run up against a bit of writer's block and I hope that coming back here I can rejuvenate and get past the block."

"Fantastic. Welcome back, and I look forward to getting to know you better, but now I had better get back to work. I have a stew cooking in the crock pot if you get hungry later, so make yourself at home and I will see you around nine," Morgan said, and then in an instant she was gone.

The aroma of the stew filled the small cabin and was making my mouth water. In my rush to escape the city I had forgotten to eat lunch and the smell of the stew made my stomach growl. I opened the refrigerator and found a large pitcher of cold water and instinctively reached into the correct cupboard for a glass. I poured a large glass and then dipped out a bowl of the stew, the gravy rich and thick accompanied by tender meat and fresh garden vegetables. There was a fresh loaf of white bread on the counter and I took out a slice to eat with the stew.

The meal was fantastic: simple, but had a better taste than most gourmet restaurants I had visited in the past few years. I used the bread to soak up the gravy in the bowl, and did not waste a drop of the precious liquid. The water, like the mountain air, was pure and tasted totally different from city water or even the best bottled water you could buy, and I drank two glasses with the meal.

After washing up my dishes, I walked outside to the base of the tower and looked up. Two hundred and four steps awaited my feet and I eagerly began my climb. Even my morning jogs did not prepare my muscles for the exertion of the climb. I managed half the steps before I had to stop for a breather. This would definitely take some getting used to again. I was not ancient by any standards, but my legs were not used to climbing this many steps. My lungs, used to the salty air at sea level, burned, and I was glad I had given up smoking a few years ago.

Morgan heard the sound of my hiking books on the metal steps and met me at the top of the landing.

"They take some getting used to," she said with a warm smile as she held the door open for me.

"Thanks," I said. "My legs are already screaming at me, but I wanted to get a good look before the sun went down." I looked out the glass window to find golden rays of sunlight bursting through the clouds to bathe the forest in glowing hues of yellow. The view took my breath away for a moment, and I stood there gazing until Morgan broke the silence.

"Is it as beautiful as you remember?" she asked.

"Even more than I can remember," I said as I turned to see her smiling at me.

"It has been a relatively quiet fire season so far, but we haven't gotten much rain to help out either," Morgan said as I walked around the observatory.

"I was lucky during my years here to experience only two fires," I said. "One caused by a careless Boy Scout campfire and the other sparked by drunken college kids setting off fireworks on the Fourth of July." I smiled, remembering those carefree days. "We were lucky and neither did much damage."

"I hope we are that lucky this year," Morgan said.

I walked over to the counter near one of the telescopes and saw a large frame of the jigsaw puzzle Morgan had been working on. "I used to love these things," I said as I picked up the box and looked at the picture of the completed puzzle.

"Feel free to do some puzzling with me then," Morgan said. "I pick up a couple new ones each week when I go to town for groceries."

"Thanks, I would like that." I looked at my watch, which read four-thirty. "I take the morning shift at six. Correct?" I asked.

"Yes ma'am, she's all yours from six to two," Morgan answered. "The forestry service still hasn't budgeted a third night watch position, but I assured them we would climb up for a look around regularly if the danger increased or we had a bad storm," she added.

"That sounds good," I said, stifling a yawn. "I have forgotten what fresh air will do to you."

"I will try to be quiet when I come in later," Morgan said as she walked me to the door.

"Your stew was fantastic, by the way," I said, and was instantly rewarded by a broad smile.

"I am glad you liked it. Your turn tomorrow night, unless you want leftovers," she said with a wink.

"If it is as good tomorrow as it was today, I would gladly eat it again," I said as I started down the stairway.

"Later," Morgan said, and disappeared back into the tower.

The burning in my legs became more pronounced the nearer I came to the bottom of the stairway. When my feet finally touched solid ground, I peered up at the tower and saw Morgan waving at me. I guess she wanted to make sure I had made it back down in one piece without falling out from a heart attack, I mused, as I waved back and walked back inside the cabin.

I stripped out of my travel clothes and walked into the bathroom for a shower. One thing for certain had not changed around the cabin, and that was the limited supply of hot water. There would not be any luxurious twenty-minute showers this summer, I thought, as I quickly bathed my body, finishing just as the flow started to cool off. I dried and slipped into a t-shirt and some well-worn boxers and dropped the dirty clothing back in my room. The cabin had a nice television in the den area and I was surprised to find that cable had arrived in the deep woods of Franklin. During my college days, you had the choice of three local channels and on many nights they had been broadcasting the same baseball game, so I was delighted to find many more choices. Ironically, I tuned into a baseball game and settled in on the large couch to watch a few innings.

Those few innings quickly put me to sleep and I napped on the couch until I heard the door open and raised my head to see Morgan walking in.

"The couch took you prisoner, I see," she said, noting the sleep still evident in my eyes.

"I was just going to watch a few innings of a ball game and I must have drifted off," I said.

"This place has an enchanting way of putting you to sleep if you remain in one position too long," Morgan stated with a grin.

"I see now," I said as I sat up on the couch, still rubbing my eyes.

"I am going to shower off real quick and eat dinner if you would care to join me," Morgan said very innocently.

"For the shower or the meal," I said without thinking.

"Both if you would like," Morgan said, without missing a beat, and smiled as my face turned scarlet.

"I am sorry, that just blurted out," I stammered in my embarrassment. I really didn't even know where that thought came from, but it was obviously floating around in my brain.

"Not a problem," Morgan said with a chuckle. "There are fresh strawberries in the fridge. If you wash and slice them, I will make shortcakes for dessert," she said as she disappeared into the bathroom, not waiting for my reply.

I walked over to the fridge, located the strawberries, washed them under cool water in the kitchen sink, and was busy slicing them when Morgan returned from the shower. She was also dressed in a t-shirt and boxers, and went to work dipping out a bowl of stew.

"Would you care for more?" she asked.

"No, I think strawberry shortcake and a glass of milk will hold me until the morning," I replied as I finished slicing the berries. I carried them to the table and sat down while Morgan finished preparing her meal. When she walked over to the table and sat down, the fabric of her boxers rode up her thigh and a wicked red burn scar was revealed. As hard as I tried not to stare, I could not keep my eyes off the mark that ran fully across her left thigh.

Morgan reached down and covered her damaged skin, with the soft fabric of the boxers concealing the scar from view. It was obvious the scar was emotionally painful to Morgan and I wanted to kick myself. In the last hour alone I had managed to embarrass myself twice and cause an innocent young woman discomfort. My actions were so unusual for me that I started to worry if I had made a good decision in coming to this place.

"I am sorry for staring," I said in a stammering attempt to apologise.

"No problem," Morgan said. "I am slowly getting used to the shocked looks."

"Still, I have been here less than twenty-four hours and I have made you uncomfortable twice now," I said.

"Not at all. I was quite humoured by your shower comment and the scar, well, it is something I have to deal with," she stated.

"Since I am on a downward spiral here, can I ask what happened?" I said.

Morgan swallowed the bite of stew and washed it down with a drink of water.

"Last summer I was chosen to train in Colorado as a fire jumper: a fire-fighter who was airlifted above the fire to rappel down onto the ground in an effort to slow the progress of a fire." She picked up a slice of the bread and dipped it in the stew's gravy as she talked. "I was two weeks from graduating at the top of the class when a fire broke out on the mountain and we were sent up to prevent the fire's spread onto a nearby cattle ranch". She took a bite of her stew and chewed as she carefully planned her next words. "We were battling the fire and had it almost contained when the winds whipped up and we were suddenly surrounded by walls of flames."

I could feel myself on the edge of my seat as I learned forward engrossed by her story.

 "Two of my fellow classmates were victims of the smoke and the surging flames. While I was awaiting evacuation from the site, a small tree collapsed and pinned me to the ground. Two of my instructors were able to cut and lift the tree off my leg, but not before it had burned through my protective suit, and the impact had fractured my femur."

Morgan remained quiet for a few minutes and I noticed that her hand had unconsciously moved to rub across the bright scar. "After surgery to pin my leg and two skin grafts to date, I am left this ugly reminder," Morgan said. "I will still have several more grafts to undergo, but the most painful part other than losing two class mates is that it prevents me from ever being a fire jumper," she said. "The scar tissue will always be very sensitive, especially to heat, and the damage to my femur would also prevent me from receiving a medical clearance to jump."

"I am so sorry, Morgan," I said. "That must have been a terrifying experience."

"It was, but I was lucky to have survived, and I will still have a career with the Forestry Service after I graduate next spring," she said and gave me a weak smile. "So, enough about me for now, tell me something about you," Morgan said as she resumed eating her meal.

"Well, you already know I am a writer and my fourth novel is due out by the beginning of next year, but I have hit a wall with the story," I said. "I hope some fresh air and less stress will allow me to resume the writing that I once loved so much."

"This place is perfect for de-stressing," Morgan said. "As long as you don't get sick of me, there will be no one else around to put pressure on you." She smiled. "I think by now you have discovered that cell telephones don't work in this area, so mine is the only voice you will hear unless you go into town," Morgan said with a grin.

"I think I can handle that, if you can tolerate me," I said with a bashful smile.

"Only on one condition," Morgan said, surprising me with the comment.

"And that would be?" I asked.

"That you can make good coffee, because frankly mine stinks," she said very seriously, then broke into a roar of laughter.

"That I can do," I said and joined the infectious laughter.

"It's a done deal then," Morgan said with tears running down her cheeks. "Are you ready for dessert?" she asked as she stood and walked to the pantry.

"All this laughter has made me hungry," I said. "Can I help?"

"You already have sliced the strawberries, so all I need is the angel food cake and some Cool-Whip, which you can get from the fridge while you pour your milk," Morgan said as she cut two large slices from the cake and placed them in bowls. She then took a fork and mashed up the strawberry slices, creating juice from the ripe berries, and sprinkled a spoonful of sugar on top, before dipping out the sweet concoction to cover the cake.

"That looks delicious," I said as Morgan placed one of the bowls in front of me.

"Dig in," she said, and she sat at the table.

Over the next hour we engaged in harmless chat, both sharing the rather bland facts of our lives as we finished off the dessert and picked up the kitchen together. It was getting late and my alarm would be going off at five the next morning, so I said goodnight to Morgan and thanked her for the great dessert.

"I need to unwind some still, so would you mind if I turned the television on?" she asked.

"Not at all," I said. "I will be out like a light as soon as my head hits the pillow."

"Goodnight then," Morgan said, and I walked into the bedroom.

Checking the alarm, I made certain it was set for five in the morning and then crawled between the crisp, fresh sheets. For a moment, I listened for the soft hum of the television, and then drifted off to sleep.

PART TWO

I awoke the next morning at a quarter to five and reached over to silence the alarm. It was not unusual for my internal clock to go off before my alarm, and I was thankful that the noise would not be waking Morgan. I sat up on the edge of the bed and searched for slippers. The room was cool and I knew the floor would be as well. I slipped my feet into the soft lambskin of my slippers and walked to the kitchen to start the coffee. I opened the refrigerator and found a bagel, sliced it and dropped it in the toaster. I poured a glass of apple juice and placed it on the table as the bagel was toasting. The coffee was brewing and filled the room with a hearty aroma. The bagel popped up from the toaster and I placed it on a small saucer and carried it to the table, where I spread cream cheese across the top of it, and then walked back to pour a cup of coffee. I sat at the table and ate my meal in the peaceful quiet of the morning.

I noticed a small notepad on the desk and after I had finished eating. I wrote *"Good Morning, Sunshine!"* on a page and placed the notepad by the coffee pot, where Morgan would be sure to see it. I don't know what had overcome me, but I felt an intoxicating need to flirt with her. Talking with her and hearing her laughter made me feel giddy and I realised just how lonesome I had grown. I had poured my second cup of coffee and was still in front of the coffee pot when I heard moans coming from Morgan's room. The sound was eerie, and I took my coffee and walked to her bedroom door.

The moans grew louder as I approached. I stopped at the door to her room and I leaned on the doorframe and looked in. Morgan was still asleep, and from the way she writhed in the bed, I suspected she was having a bad dream. Her moans were from pain, but it was difficult to tell if they were inflicted physically or mentally. I listened and could make out the name Meagan as I watched tears stream down Morgan's cheeks. I contemplated waking her to break her dream, then thought better of my decision and left her to finish her dream. I dressed quickly and quietly brushed my teeth and hair before stepping out into a cool morning.

The namesake mist of the Smokeys hung thick and shrouded the tower. Standing at the base and looking up, I could only see half of the metal steps that disappeared into the mist. There wouldn't be much to see, but I should be able to get some writing done before the mist burnt off and the sun illuminated the beautiful mountains. I shouldered my laptop bag and started the climb, silently counting each of the steps. The muscles of my legs felt tight and stiff as each step echoed in the cool morning air.

I refused to allow myself to stop, forcing my legs to rise and fall all the way to the top. I was breathing deeply by the time I reached the top and surprised to find I had broken a light sweat in the coolness. I reached for the handle that was cold in my hand and wished I had remembered a jacket or sweatshirt. When I opened the door, I was bathed in warmth, a complete surprise. In the centre of the room there was a small heater, pouring out electric warmth and filling the room with a soft glow.

I smiled as I walked over to the counter and placed my laptop bag on its surface. On a notepad by the lamp was a handwritten note from Morgan which read:

Welcome Home! I hope you have a fantastic first day back in the tower. I will bring lunch up around noon. I hope you like egg salad

M

Egg salad was one of my favourite sandwiches, but there was no way Morgan could have known that. There was something special about that woman, and it stirred desires that I hadn't felt in ages. Those feelings both terrified and excited me as I began my first morning in the tower.

I eagerly set up my laptop, and within minutes the words began to flow and it felt... good. Thirty more minutes had expired before I looked up from the keyboard to see that the sun was beginning to burn through the mist and light the forest. I stood and took a walk around the observatory. Most of the woods were still shrouded in mist, but, where the sun's rays were burning through, they coated the leaves with a golden hue.

I stopped in front of the counter that held the jigsaw puzzle, and could not resist picking up a piece and turning it in my fingers until my eye located the spot where it fitted perfectly and my fingers snapped it in place. I walked over to where I had been sitting at the laptop and pressed the button on a small timer that began a countdown from thirty minutes. Then, I walked back to the puzzle and looked at the cover again—it showed a beautiful picture of the Stone Arches of Moab, Utah. I sat down in the chair that Morgan had spent countless hours in and I began to puzzle.

When the timer went off, I was startled by the sound. I had been concentrating on the puzzle so intensely that I had lost track of the passing of time. I stood and made rounds, noting the sun was lighting up over half the valley as the shadows were slowly disappearing.

The flashing of the cursor brought my attention back to the laptop and after setting the timer I sat down and began typing again. I spent the remainder of the morning composing the first chapter of my novel and was busy proofreading when I heard the rhythmic thump, thump of Morgan's boots as she climbed the stairs to the tower. As her steps grew louder, I stood and walked to the door to meet her.

"Hello," Morgan said as she looked up, and saw me waiting for her.

"Can I help with anything?" I asked.

"No, Jordan, I have it under control," she said.

"Egg salad is my favourite," I said, my mouth watering for the taste.

"I made a good choice then," Morgan said as she reached the top. "I hope you like sweet baby gherkins too," she said with a chuckle.

"And a pitcher of sweet tea—my Lord, I have died and gone to heaven," I said.

"It's the least I could do in appreciation of finally drinking a decent cup of coffee," Morgan said.

"I will make you coffee every morning then," I said.

"I couldn't ask for a better deal," she said as she walked to the counter and sat the tray down.

She took the plastic wrap off a stack of sandwiches, cut in half, and popped the lid on the pickle jar as I poured two glasses of tea. Morgan glanced over at the laptop.

"Having any luck?" she asked.

"Not bad so far," I said as I sat next to her, and bit into a sandwich and moaned in appreciation.

"Now, that sound is heaven to my ears," Morgan said with a devilish grin.

I thought of the moans coming from Morgan's room earlier this morning, but did not think it was a good time to mention them.

"This is the best egg salad I have ever eaten," I said as I finished off the first half of a sandwich.

"I am glad you are enjoying it," Morgan said.

"I took some pork chops out of the freezer this morning that I thought I would bake with some macaroni and cheese and fresh green beans if that's good with you," I said.

"That would be fantastic," she said as she slowly chewed her food. I noticed Morgan was rubbing her thigh as she ate.

"Are you hurting today?" I asked.

"We are going to get rain in the next few days," she said. "Since the accident, I always know when it is coming."

"Maybe you should consider a career in weather forecasting," I said with a grin.

"That might not be a bad idea at all," Morgan said, returning my grin. "The dull ache I get is much more reliable and accurate than most of the forecasts you see on the television," she said. "I can guarantee that we will have rain within the next two days."

"I hope you are correct, we sure could use the rain," I said. "I don't know about you, but I love a nice gentle rain, especially at night on the tin roof of the cabin. Makes me sleep like a baby."

"I could use a good night's sleep," Morgan said.

"You have trouble sleeping?" I asked.

"I couldn't tell you when I last had a full night of sleep," Morgan said.

I blushed and Morgan asked, "Why are you blushing?"

"When I was drinking coffee this morning, I heard you moaning and when I went to look in on you, you appeared to be dreaming, clutching your pillow and you called out a name," I said.

"Meagan?" she asked.

I blushed again and nodded my head yes.

Morgan was silent for several minutes before she looked me in the eyes; the green eyes that sparkled so bright were full of tears. "Meagan and I were lovers for two years. She was one of the two fire jumpers that were killed on the mountain that day," she said with tears rolling down her cheeks. "We were running up the mountain to the evacuation point when she collapsed from smoke inhalation and as I turned to help her onto her feet, the tree fell, pinning us both to the hot ground." Morgan stood and walked across the room. She looked out the window and took a deep breath before she continued the story. "Our instructors returned to attempt a rescue, using chainsaws to cut the tree off of our bodies, but it was too late for Meagan." Morgan broke down in sobs. "She died in my arms."

I stood up and walked over to Morgan and wrapped my arms around her and held her close. Her body was wracked with hard sobs as she mourned her lost love. Our bodies rocked together slowly until she was able to control her tears and she looked up to me with bloodshot eyes. "Thank you," she whispered.

I leaned down and kissed the top of her head and hugged her close.

"I needed to get that out of my system," she said. "Almost every night I dream of her and until now, no one ever knew that she and I were lovers."

I stepped back from her and looked her directly in her eyes.

"Thank you for sharing that with me," I said. "That gives me perspective on how you felt about Meagan and the tremendous loss you have experienced."

"It was the most difficult time of my life," Morgan said. "My injury prevented me from attending her funeral and I feel like I have no sense of closure—my mind just will not let her go," she said as she began to cry again.

I reached out to her and she stepped into my arms, pulling me close, clinging to me desperately as her body purged the tears she had held in for so long. I had no words to comfort her and I felt completely inadequate to help Morgan deal with her grief, so I held on to her for dear life.

Morgan cried until she had no tears left and when she stepped back, she seemed different, a little more relaxed, and there seemed to be a different sparkle in her eyes. She looked at me and cocked her head to the side and smiled at me. No words passed between us, just that look and that smile and I felt my heart melting. I desperately wanted to take Morgan into my arms and kiss her at that moment, but I would not take advantage of her vulnerability. If we were to share a kiss it needed to be initiated by Morgan, when she felt the time was right for her to move on.

Sensing my interest and my hesitance, Morgan turned back to the table.

"I guess I had better get moving if I am going to be relieving you at two," she said. Morgan picked up the tray and before I could think of any words to speak, she was out the door and moving quickly down the steps.

I sighed, confused about what had just transpired between us, and spent the remainder of my shift trying to sort out my scattered thoughts. I looked at the computer and sat down in front of it, opening up a new file and started typing what I was feeling, my fingers flying across the keys with a will of their own. I don't remember thinking the words that came to life on the computer's screen and when my thoughts were finished I scrolled back to the top and began reading. When I got to the bottom of the third and final page, my thoughts were crystal clear. I was about to type the final three words when I heard Morgan come rushing up the stairs. I quickly saved the file and shut down the computer, suddenly embarrassed by the thoughts I was having, and closed the computer lid just as Morgan came through the door.

"Welcome back," I said to Morgan.

She walked directly over to me and hugged me close. I could smell the fragrance of the shampoo in her hair, still damp from the shower. I felt a shiver run through my body, even though my blood was on fire.

"Are you cold?" she asked.

"Just a quick shiver," I said and quickly turned away. "See you at nine?"

"My mouth is already watering for pork chops," she said as she watched me walk towards the door.

"I will have dinner ready then," I said as I slipped out the door and made my way down the steps.

The warm sunshine felt marvellous on my skin as I descended from the tower. The day had blossomed into a beautiful afternoon and, reluctant to return inside, I decided to walk down the lane to the mailbox, even though I doubted there would be any mail inside. I was halfway down the lane when I heard movement in the bushes to my right. I froze in my tracks and waited until a pair of chipmunks came scurrying across my path, stopping only momentarily to give me a once-over before chattering to each other and disappearing into bushes on the other side of the lane.

When I reached the end of the lane I looked down the desolate blacktop and found it empty in both directions. The road was rarely used and the only sounds carried through the air were the calling of birds and the bellowing of a cow in search of a wayward calf. Life seemed so simple, the air sweet and clean and my heart lost to the woman making rounds in the observatory several hundred yards away. How was I to proceed, I wondered, as I walked slowly back to the cabin.

I looked into the sink and the pork chops had fully thawed, so I placed them in the refrigerator and walked towards my room. I decided to take a nap and then shower before starting dinner, so I stripped off my clothes and walked to the bathroom. The shower was very relaxing and when I had dried I was ready for a nap. I didn't bother with clothing and stretched out on top of the bed. Looking out the window I could see the top of the tower and I wondered what Morgan was doing. The way her green eyes sparkled at me made me smile and I found my hands softly stroking my skin as I closed my eyes and imagined Morgan's hands caressing me. My nipples grew hard as my fingertips circled them slowly and I felt my body responding, moisture growing between my thighs.

It had been over a year since I had allowed myself to feel the pleasure that was coursing through my veins at the moment and my body was eagerly responding to the attention. My hands caressed further down my body, stroking the inside of my thighs as a climax began to build in the core of my being. The fingertips of my left hand gently parted my lips and I could feel my clit as it continued to swell with excitement, becoming engorged with blood.

Morgan stopped dead in her tracks as she made her rounds. She looked down at the cabin and nearly fainted when she looked into

Jordan's bedroom window and saw her lying naked on the bed. She was mesmerised by the beauty of Jordan's body and she felt her heart drop to her stomach as she watched Jordan's hands as they teased and stimulated her body. She could feel her wetness growing as she watched Jordan's hips rocking to a sensual rhythm as her fingers slid in and out of her body.

My body shook with delight as my fingers delved deeper with each thrust of my hips. My breath was caught in my throat as the first wave of orgasm passed through my body and continued for several minutes.

Morgan was transfixed by the complete rapture on Jordan's face as she climaxed and she wished for a moment she were there to hear the soft moans of pleasure she was sure Jordan was experiencing. The timer chose that moment to go off, startling Morgan back to reality. She moved to restart the timer and sat at the puzzle as she tried to erase the visions of Jordan from her mind.

My body relaxed in complete satisfaction and I quickly drifted into slumber, still lying naked on the bed. I slept for two hours then ran back through the shower before dressing and starting dinner. I placed the pork chops in the oven to allow them to bake slowly and went to the den to watch some television. I would start the rest of the meal at eight and have everything piping hot when Morgan came down from the tower.

PART THREE

I was placing the last of the dishes on the table when I heard Morgan's boots on the porch and a few seconds later she walked through the door. Her eyes lit up at the table full of food and she rewarded me with a brilliant smile.

"My, that sure does look good," she said. "Let me go wash up and I will be right back," Morgan said as she slipped into the bathroom to wash her hands.

I poured two glasses of tea and was seated at the table when she returned.

"Dig in," I said as she took a seat.

We ate the meal over light conversation and when she could eat no more, Morgan pushed her chair back from the table.

"I will die if I eat another bite," she declared.

"You better stop then," I said with a satisfied smile.

"If you plan on cooking like this every night, I better find my running shoes and take up jogging again," Morgan said.

The image of a hot and sweaty Morgan flashed before my eyes and I felt my face go hot. Morgan noticed too and gave me a curious look, but did not comment.

"Why don't you take a shower and I will do the dishes," I suggested.

"You have a deal ma'am, if you are sure I can't help," she said.

"I have most of them done already, so it won't take but a minute," I said.

"I will see you soon then," Morgan said and walked from the room.

I finished cleaning the kitchen and walked back to the den and lay down on the couch to watch the movie playing on the screen while Morgan finished showering. When she walked into the room and sat on the edge of the couch I moved to sit up and she reached out to stop me.

"Stay where you are," Morgan said.

"No, I need to quit hogging the couch," I said.

"Well, I was hoping that you would hold me again," Morgan said.

I smiled and moved backwards on the couch and rolled onto my side.

"Join me then," I said.

Morgan shifted and lay down beside me, facing the television and scooting her body back into mine while she placed her head on my outstretched arm under the pillow. I wrapped my left arm around her waist and held her close to my body. The smell of her clean hair and the warmth of her body next to mine was pure torture. I lay my head next to hers and breathed in her scent as I pretended to watch the movie. We lay there in silence, sharing the comfort of one another until the movie ended.

Morgan turned the television off and rolled over on the couch and lay facing me. Our lips were mere inches apart. My tongue snaked out to wet my lips and Morgan smiled softly. She leaned forward and closed her eyes as our lips met, softly brushing in a tender kiss. The kiss lasted for only a few seconds and then Morgan reached up to stroke my cheek.

"Sleep with me tonight," she whispered softly. "No expectations, but I could use your company tonight."

I nodded my head and Morgan stood and, taking my hand, led me into her bedroom. She pulled back the covers and climbed into the bed and reached for my hand to pull me in close behind her. I snuggled my body close to hers and pulled the covers over our bodies. I wrapped my arm around her waist and this time she took my hand in hers, holding it gently.

My body was soaring with desire as we lay so close in the bed, but I was content in holding Morgan close. I was about to whisper goodnight when I heard her softly purring as she slept. With a smile frozen on my face I held her while she slept and the comfortable warmth of her body enticed me to join her in sleep.

Around three in the morning, I awoke, still wrapped around Morgan's body. I could see the soft smile playing on her face as she slept and my ears picked up a faint sound coming from outside. I looked at the window to discover small rivers of raindrops sliding down the glass panes. The raindrops reminded me of the tears Morgan had shed that day and her promise of a coming rain. Her prediction was correct; I listened to the rain gently pelting the tin roof with a smile gracing on my face.

I felt Morgan shift her body, and when I looked back from the window she was watching me.

"I told you so," she softly whispered.

"I never doubted you for a second," I said.

Morgan moved closer to me, our bodies touching, and she lifted her hand to softly stroke my face. Her fingers felt so soft against my skin and her touch made my body tingle with excitement. Her eyes searched mine, looking for an answer to an unspoken question, the silence hanging in the air between us.

"Jordan," she whispered, calling my name.

I leaned down and brushed her lips with mine, a soft kiss that lingered only briefly as I raised my head to look into her eyes. Her eyes were glowing like emerald gems as she pulled my head back down and she kissed me. Morgan's tongue penetrated my lips, gently sliding into my mouth and I could taste the sweetness of her tongue as it swirled slowly inside my mouth. She rolled me onto my back as the kiss grew deeper and when she draped her left leg over my thigh and rested part of her weight on me, my body was consumed by her passion. The heat between us soared like the flames of a forest fire, her kiss stealing the oxygen from my lungs, fuelling the desire between us. My hand slid beneath her shirt, fingertips slowly dragging up her spine as her left hand found my right breast, teasing my nipple through the fabric of my shirt, and I arched my back, eager for her touch. My body ached to feel Morgan's skin, and I slowly worked her shirt up her back until she broke our kiss and pulled it over her head, tossing it to the floor. She raised my shirt and removed it and devoured my body with her bright eyes before leaning down to continue the kiss. Her skin was hot on my body as her fire burned into me, igniting an uncontrollable lust in me. I used my hands to pull her hips and bring her body fully on top of me, my hands tugging at her hips as I ground my hips into hers. Moans filled the room, and I could not separate mine from hers, our mouths and bodies locked together in a sensual dance, oblivious to anything but the need between us. Her hands had covered my breasts, kneading them as her hips rolled rhythmically between my drenched thighs.

My hands caressed from her hips to her breasts, the soft flesh hot to my touch and her nipples hard, and my mouth ached to kiss them. With an aggressive move, I rolled Morgan onto her back and covered her body with mine as I began to lick and kiss my way down her neck, my fingers rolling her nipples between my fingers. This time I was certain it was Morgan's moans that filled the room as her eyes watched intently, and my mouth inched its way down to her right breast. I flicked my tongue out to lightly brush across her nipple and Morgan reached out to bury her hand in my hair as she pulled my mouth down onto her breast. I could feel her wetness soak through her boxers as my mouth feasted on her breast. My teeth raked over her nipple, as my right hand lowered Morgan's boxers down her hips as she raised them off the bed. I removed my boxers and we were completely skin to skin.

Morgan's nails trailed up and down my back as I suckled her breast. I could feel her wetness, silky and hot against my skin and I knew I had to taste her soon or I would explode. My fingers crept between her thighs, bathing in the drops of wetness covering her soft curls. I could feel her clit as it peeked out from its protective cover, hot to the touch and begging for attention.

Unable to restrain myself further, I moved down the bed until I rested between Morgan's legs, the width of my shoulders spreading her thighs. My fingers opened her lips as my tongue traced the ridges of her lips and her sweet taste erupted in my mouth. It was my turn to moan loudly as my body soared with excitement as I drank from Morgan's body.

Her fingers clutched the sheets as my tongue slipped inside her, delving deep inside her wetness as I lapped up her juices. My tongue swirled and caressed, as my thumb slowly circled her throbbing clit until she cried out and arched her hips, filling my mouth with a rush of liquid heaven. Two of my fingers penetrated her deeply as my mouth closed over her clit, sucking it against the roof of my mouth and I loved her slowly until she shuddered and came again. The inner walls of her muscles constricted around my fingers as spasms pulsed through her body. I softly kissed her clit and gently removed my fingers as she lay gasping for breath.

I lay my head on her thigh as I tried to regain my breath as well and my fingers reached over to touch the angry red skin of her scar. Morgan reached over to pull the sheet over her thigh to hide the damaged flesh and I gently, but firmly, pushed her hand aside. My fingers traced the contours of her skin and I softly kissed the raised surface of the scar that caused her so much pain.

I looked up to find Morgan looking at me, tears trailing down her cheeks like the raindrops sliding down the window panes. I climbed back up to lie beside her on the bed and folded her into my arms, holding her close as she wept.

She rested her head on my shoulder, and I could feel the pounding of her heart in her chest. My hand softly stroked her hair as her tears continued to fall. When Morgan tears abated, she raised her head from my shoulder to speak, but I placed a finger to her lips.

"Shh, not now," I said. "Just relax and listen."

We lay there, wrapped in each other's bodies, listening to the gently falling rain until sleep captured us again. I woke a few hours later and crept from the bed to start the coffee and crawled back in bed to snuggle Morgan awake.

So began our summer, and the love we shared flourished, growing every day. My novel sprung to life in the fire tower and the draft was finished in record time. I knew this one would be my best so far, and we drove to town together to mail it off to my editor. I had indeed rejuvenated my writing, but more importantly, I had found a love like no other, one that consumed my heart, and when the summer ended I sold my home in the city and bought a beautiful cabin near a mountain top. My love returned to school and by the spring she had graduated and was now my Ranger Montgomery.

Morgan had one other skin graft on her leg and then was content that she would carry the remainder of the damage for life. The red, distorted skin would serve as a constant reminder of her strength and courage and the love she had shared with Meagan.

Sometimes, on hot summer nights, we still ride out to the fire tower and climb to the top to sit and gaze out at the stars gracing the night sky as we reminisce over the first summer we shared together.

Four years and six novels later, we continue to live happily together.

A PHILADELPHIA STORY

by

Melody Breyer-Grell

Melody Breyer-Grell has been active in the creative arts since childhood.
This classically trained opera singer turned to jazz and has put out an
award winning debut CD – 'The Right Time'. Melody chronicled the ups and downs of pursuing music in the hysterical 'What's Funny about Jazz? - A Show for Nobody'.

Grell's song lyrics helped her secure and become a senior contributor (interviews, features and reviews) for Cabaret Scenes Magazine. Melody is a prolific contributor to 'The Huffington Post' and made her fiction debut in Freya Publication's anthology, 'SunKissed'.

Staff meetings were a brief Monday morning affair at "The Colonial", a French-Asian fusion restaurant in the heart of Philadelphia's Center City, sort of a mini-Manhattan in the "City of Brotherly Love". It was 1982, Disco was hot, and the twenty-five year old Moira was lucky enough to be holding down the position of sous-chef in this popular middle-scale bistro. Moira, a born cook, loved her job for the most part, but found the meetings tedious and repetitive. They were held between breakfast and the lunch rush. She spent most of her time looking at her watch, waiting for it to be over so she could get out the prep for lunch, not that Monday was all that busy.

Moira, named after Moira Shearer, the Irish ballet dancer and movie star, had little in common with the Irish icon, excepting her red hair, a not uncommon trait to that ethnicity. Other than that, Moira was a bit muscular, freckled and only about 5'4". She was cute as a puppy and always demanded to wear pants instead of a dress. A hard to control dynamo, by four years old she already "baked" her first cake by spilling open a sack of flour, breaking a dozen eggs on the floor and proudly showing her work to her Ma.

"Look Mama, cake!" she cooed proudly, her curly hair and face covered with flour.

This was not her first interest in food production as she scaled the pantry cabinets of their Upper Manhattan brownstone, finding all the canned foods, ripping off the labels, causing many a surprise supper for the Connors family.

She was more mischievous than any of her three older brothers were, and Ma had to clean up the mess before Da came home and threatened her with his belt. An idle threat it was, for as Da quoted, "When she was good, she was very, very good, but when she was bad she was horrid." Her parents adored their tomboy, first-generation American, and she was constantly informed she could take on the world and succeed at anything she wanted to.

Moira succeeded in getting her wish to attend the CIA ("what, are you gonna have a gun?" her brother Tom teased) better known as the Culinary Institute of America. Her mind was always on cooking, especially loving the simple things: peeling a bag of potatoes in ten minutes, chopping two bags of carrots into five. It was her form of religion, a meditation, as such. Her parents, upon realizing that she was not college-bound, ended up giving her their blessing, acknowledging that her passion was the knife and not the pen.

She also discovered that she was different from most other girls. During camp trips to The Bronx's Orchard Beach, what intrigued her most was having an opportunity to steal peeks at her counsellor's bare breasts as they changed in the locker room. She also experienced her first heartbreak when the girl she fancied was removed from her side and relegated to a different seat on the bus. She cried for an hour, hating so to be separated from the pretty dark-haired camp mate. The counsellors had no idea why this overreaction and just let the eight-year-old cry it out.

Moira started to really understand the lay of the land a few years later when she had a secret crush on her high school musical's "leading lady." The budding lesbian did not make a move on the swan-like ingénue, but she did sneak into as many rehearsals as she could. She was starting to know what gay was and she was indeed gay—something that she was not comfortable enough yet to share with her high school cohorts.

At eighteen she was seduced (willingly) by a married pastry instructor at the CIA. She went in hungry for experience, but also knowing however gratifying the affair was, she was merely a conquest and her teacher was never going to leave her husband, for her or any other girl. She also knew that she was not going to be a pastry chef either, as her interests were completely "savoury".

After a couple of years working in New York City she landed a position as managing Sous Chef in Philadelphia.

Philly was something else, probably the gayest town after "The Big Apple", or at least it seemed so to Moira. She had a succession of brief encounters, never finding that right girl to settle down with, and at the ripe old age of twenty-five she was getting worried. The sex was always good, but she found many of the girls were highly neurotic, boring, or really looking for a man.

Most of the staff meetings at The Colonial were short, terse, and littered with complaints: too much waste, food cost had gone up, there was a recession, blah blah blah. But this meeting was something quite different.

"We are adding some new staff," announced executive chef Jim Beavers. His employees got a kick out of that name, for sure. Maybe the name made him mean—he was one hell of a curmudgeon.

The re-staffing in itself was not terribly surprising. The summer was almost over and the return of students to their various schools —U. of Penn or Music and Art—created a deficit. Not that Moira would miss most of them. As a manager, she really had to work on her temper when these "temps" would not ever even try to save on produce or properly season the mayonnaise.

"Hey Stu, you're not supposed to remove ten layers of onion before dicing them. Don't cry, I am not yelling," she joked, to take the edge off her reprimand.

"Rita, can you put those turkeys in the walk-in before they fly away?"

Moira was either loved or disliked by her co-workers. She had a great sense of humour but was serious about things that other people did not get. She intimidated some of the students, but others had secret crushes on her. Sadly it was mostly the men who made these crushes clear. There was a spate of women who liked her but she usually missed the signals, even when one of them asked her if she wanted a massage.

In any case, today's meeting's big announcement was that the restaurant was making seven new hires, and that they were all from Thailand.

Moira groused somewhat insensitively, "Do they even speak English?" It was hard enough teaching the college kids how to clean spinach properly.

Beavers glared at her, stating, "I know you will help them, won't you." It was not a question.

She tried not to talk back to Jim, because as much as he admired her in the kitchen he found her a general pain in the butt. She always had a fear that she would be fired because of her "intense nature".

She also had something else on her mind. She had developed an unlikely crush on Joanie. Unlikely because, even though also gay, the woman was not that attractive and had nothing in common with Moira. Joanie hated her job and just did it as a way to make money so she could do her "art". Her art (which she had presented at a grungy loft that past spring) consisted of triangles, just triangles of all sizes and colours but nothing else. A tall, gangly brunette, she was not pretty, or sporty, but had sad brown eyes that Moira knew she would put a twinkle in if allowed entrance into the woman's life.

"What do you see in her?" asked Ronnie, her male counterpart at work. "She isn't at all hot, you can do much better. Look at her skin."

"So she is a little broken out—I don't know, I just kinda want to make her happy, I know I could light her up like a Christmas tree. All she needs is a night with me! I'm gonna get her. I'll clear that skin up! She is coming to the dance at The Bar on Friday." "Sneakers", one of the only lesbian bars in Philly, was just referred to as "The Bar", since there was not much else going on. There might be a ton of dykes in town, but they did not drink enough to fill the coffers—at least, that was the general consensus.

Friday was also when the Thai invasion started. A smiling and friendly group, although they spoke no English, they were very comfortable in the 100-degree kitchen. Most were male youths in their early- to mid-20s, but there were a couple of females, including one matriarchal-looking woman in her forties, a stone faced statue that all the "kids" seemed to answer to.

Moira met the other woman, really a girl almost—Mali, her new assistant. Distracted enough not to notice her delicate stature, perfect skin and lovely smile, Boss Lady just testily asked her if she knew what lettuce was.

"Ah, leteece?"

This was going to be a real pain in the ass, Moira thought, as she mimed out the instructions to the nervous new Asian.

"There are three types of lettuce," she explained, holding up three fingers and pointing to the boxes, "that need to be washed and chopped in the giant metal sink on the left wall of the kitchen. Is very dirty, you need to clean three times." Again with the fingers.

Moira returned to her list of prep work, pulled out a five-pound bunch of fresh carrots, removed their tops, tossed them in the ever-simmering stock pot, and started peeling furiously. Then it was time for some real cooking. But before she was even finished boning a half dozen ducks, she received a timid poke from Mali, indicating that she had finished with the lettuce.

If lettuce preparation could be impressive, Mali's certainly was. She washed it more thoroughly (and got out all the grit) than any newbie ever had and chopped it neatly, leaving no long strays. She had figured out to put the roughage in the large plastic bins, and the sink was clean for the next task.

"Very good," nodded the sous-chef as her new charge beamed proudly. In the next few hours Mali picked up more knife technique than the most fêted U. of Penn student. She did not have to be shown anything twice.

Still distracted by the lethargic Joanie standing across the large metal table, Moira was obsessing about the night and how she was going to seduce her.

Many of the kitchen staff were interested in the Thai chefs (they really were skilled) and their culture, attempting to teach them English, while picking up some Thai themselves.

Moira had to race against the clock, for however fast she was there was always more to do than time permitted, being that she did not trust the night staff, who she was sure goofed off half the time.

Finishing off her list by boiling a tremendous vat of tiny pasta for orzo, carrot and raisin salad, she carefully placed the colander in the sink, rinsing and lightly oiling it so it would not stick together. The steam of the process created a clean sweat on her face and she towelled it down while checking the clock. It was 3:55, the shift ending at 4:00 officially—but Moira usually had 20 minutes more work to do before she could comfortably leave the kitchen, confident that those lazy night-people would be equipped to carry out the work plan.

Once again she felt a little tug from Mali and was fairly astonished by what she saw. Neatly lined up on the metal tables were four tremendous bins of vegetables, fruits and garnishes.

Crafted slender julienned carrots (rather than the rough finger-sized ones that were produced by the summer crowd), evenly cubed red peppers and an array of polished radish garnish—the list went on. They were finished, there was literally nothing for the night people to do except to take prepared dishes and send them up to the serving line.

The shift over, Moira hastily thanked Mali. She hurriedly turned her attention to an apathetic Joanie in the locker room, as they changed into street clothes.

"See ya at the bar tonight?"

"Yeah, sure."

"Oh good, what time, around 9?"

"Okay, yeah, around 9."

"Cool."

Nancy, the restaurant's personal yenta, was listening in on the terse conversation. An older, twice-divorced woman, Nancy really rubbed Moira up the wrong way, fast with the gossip and slow with the knife. She did not know why they kept her on, but she guessed it was about having some people who were more "mature". She thought she was the devil and ignored her unless she had to discuss some work-related business.

"So what's up with you and Joanie?" Nancy wheedled.

"Gotta run, see ya!" Moira evaded.

"That new girl is nice, huh? She tries so hard…"

Moira was already out the door…

Luckily, Moira lived in a large, sparsely-furnished loft around the corner from the restaurant. She jumped into the shower and washed her hair the minute she returned home. She made some popcorn (the chef never cooked at home anymore) and put some Bach on her turntable. The one course she liked in High School was music appreciation. She originally took it as an easy-A goof course, but was soon caught up in the different moods and inexplicable emotions that emanated from classical music.

With the sounds of Bach soothing her clean body she dozed lightly on her crimson velveteen couch anticipating her Friday night out.

The bar was quite a different scene than Moira's relaxing, Bach-filled apartment. She did not much mind the crowds and noise and was even excited by the charge she felt from women with women. Moira did get depressed sometimes, in that that she was not in a real relationship. She honestly did not even expect one with Joanie. In a rare moment of deeper reflection she wondered why she always picked losers to go after. Was she afraid of the real thing?

She "got out of her head" when she saw Joanie coming her way. At least Joanie made an effort to look good that night. Her tall androgynous body was outfitted with a nice crisp man-shirt and her jeans suited her just fine. She had combed back her usually messy short hair and was quite dapper, a bit like a dark David Bowie. Moira was getting turned on. She wanted to touch Joanie, tell her what fun they could have if they got to know each other…

"Hey, do you want a Rolling Rock (a popular beer in Philly at the time, before microbreweries and whatnot)," offered Moira.

"Sure."

They both downed two bottles each and Joanie seemed to cheer up in a way that did not seem possible at work. Things were looking good.

The D.J. blasted Bowie's *Let's Dance* and Moira pulled her intended out on the dance floor. They danced for about 45 minutes and Moira felt her desire mounting as the set finished with Blondie's *Rapture*.

The girls went back to the bar for a couple more "Rocks", and while Joanie was sitting on the stool waiting to order, Moira stealthily leaned down, kissing her straight on the mouth... She felt some reciprocal response, and Joanie did not pull away.

Before you could say blue balls, a couple of co-workers—Jenny and Beth—spun around them, winked, and started talking shop. Philly was a small city and the lesbian world was very incestuous, everybody being in everyone's personal business.

"Hey guys!" Moira said, a bit drunkenly. The third beer had worked a magical buzz on both the women, but the arrival of Jenny and Beth had broken the mood.

Eventually, Joanie apologetically begged off with an, "I don't feel that great, why don't you hang, I am going to go home."

Feeling thwarted, but not hopeless (she knew Joanie liked the kiss) Moira walked Joanie to the doors.

"Are you sure you don't want me to take you home—you don't feel good, maybe…"

"No, I will be fine once I lie down—just tired."

"Okay, see you Monday."

Damn.

She hung around a bit more with Jen and Beth, shooting the breeze about the new hires. Sobering up quickly and feeling bored, Moira excused herself and walked home. She did not take cabs; in fact, she started saving up as soon as she got her first job. She did not want to be a renter forever, houses were cheap in Philly, and her father always said real estate was the best investment a person could make. He should know: he owned the brownstone they lived in and had seen it triple in value since he acquired it some twenty-seven years ago.

"Remember girl, real estate, that's the ticket."

"Yes, okay. Da, you are starting to sound like the father in *Gone with the Wind*." She mimicked his still-strong Irish accent.

But she did take his advice and squirreled away all she could manage.

The following Monday, Joanie came in to work and flashed Moira an enigmatic smile, but no words were passed. The week flew by, and another, and another. The girls went out a couple more times with mostly the same results, one kiss and that was it. Joanie let Moira know that she was deeply depressed when her college girlfriend and she parted after graduation—she really had not recovered. This was not encouraging news, but Moira was still on her mission.

In the meantime, Mali was turning out to be a miracle. She was picking up some English, but more importantly she was taking quite a load off Moira's shoulders. She learned from the others that Mali was a "nun" in Thailand, but did not figure out if it was a temporary thing or permanent, as for the Catholics. Some of the more adventurous people were planning on taking a trip to Thailand when vacation time came during the upcoming holidays.

Moira had no interest in going to Thailand, but started feeling a strange affection for the girl. She had come in late a few times and found that all the lunch prep had been done and the girl was smiling broadly, looking for approval. It was cute.

To show her appreciation Moira took Mali to a special management dinner at a new restaurant the boss was opening. Some people were looking at them strangely but Moira took did not notice. She was too busy trying to make some conversation with the girl who giggled and blushed a lot for a "nun."

The next day she saw Mali and the Matriarch in some sort of argument. Moira did not understand a world of it, but she saw the older woman stare at her sideways. Mali was standing her ground, but whatever they were talking about was intense. Maybe they are just an emotional people, like Italians, giggled Moira to herself, not really thinking much about the melee.

Finally, Moira was able to persuade Joanie to agree to come visit her apartment for dinner. Though she rarely cooked at home, she would prepare a stuffed veal that she had perfected at work. It would be served with wild rice, fresh asparagus tips and the Rolling Rocks would be replaced by some white wine.

Upon arrival, Joanie showed up looking more nervous than usual but relaxed after drinking several glasses of wine. Moira was starting to believe that the woman might be an alcoholic. The veal turned out well and they looked for things to talk about, Moira always taking the lead.

Finally, slowly, Moira moved next to Joanie and beckoned her to the couch.

She kissed her lips, gently and then with more pressure. They were soon ripping each other's clothes off, Moira gently lowering her body on Joanie's, rubbing her breasts, going lower, climaxing, both women falling asleep in each other's arms.

When Moira woke up she was surprised to see that Joanie was already dressed and combing her hair. She felt her elation replaced by trepidation.

"Joanie, I want you to listen to this."

Impulsively, Moira threw Beethoven's 9th on her record player, convinced that it would rekindle what had seemed to have burned out so quickly.

Inspired by the music Moira became almost manic and danced around the room, finally grabbing Joanie, kissing her vigorously, and attempting to cup both her breasts.

Joanie yanked herself away and put her hands over her head.

"Can't you see it?" she cried. All this music, the food, you…"

"Don't say you are not attracted to me, not after what just happened tonight!"

"You don't get it. Sure, I am attracted to you, but I do not want to be with you or any other woman. It doesn't work, women can't be together. There is no future."

"Why do you say that, that is just your depression talking!" Moira was now crying with frustration and anger.

"That music to you, you love it, right? To me it is just background music. You love to cook; everything you do is touched with passion. I am not that person, but you are. You will find someone, you will be happy—you are open, I am closed. I am finished here… I am joining the army; I was going to tell you tonight."

"Why?" Moira started, but she knew she was defeated. "Don't let's leave like this, I get it, I get it. There is nothing with us, just sex. I pushed it. Okay, I get it. Let me make us some coffee, I don't want our goodbye to be so upsetting."

They quietly sipped their coffee and said their goodbyes with a limp hug.

"Sorry," said Joanie.

"No, it's nothing; I guess I knew it could never have worked out. I did think we could have some fun though. Take care—say hello to Uncle Sam for me."

That was the last she saw of Joanie, and after a week of sighing and moaning and analysing, Moira let go of her infatuation. The real question was why did she bother? If she just wanted sex, she could find it elsewhere. Why pick the sad-sacks?

At work things were heating up. The guys were getting excited by their plan to go to Thailand.

Mali, as always was working harder and harder, pushing her tiny self beyond need.

"Hey 'Li, take it easy," Moira smiled. "We are in good shape." They were stacking 20 quarts of fresh cream sauce in the walk-in.

Mali grabbed Moira's arm urgently.

"Need to say someting, I to you—need to say—ask you, *koon ben gai*?"

"What? Yes I *gai*, me *koon gai*," Moira laughed back, not quite sure of what the girl was so urgent about.

"*Pom ben gai, pom ben gai*," the girl urged on.

"Whatever. Yes, whatever you say."

"Wite me pleaz wite me—Enlish betta now."

"Okay," she humoured the girl, "I will write you," never asking her address because they were all coming back in two weeks anyway.

Mali was still babbling incoherently.

"Let's get out of here, it's cold! Out!" Moira gently tugged the girl outside of the box.

The next day Mali was even more ardent in her pleadings:

"*Gai, gai!*" she insisted.

Moira saw a chilling look directed to her on the Thai Matriarch's face.

"What is up with that bag?" Moira thought, but she did not yet have a clue.

The whole staff was getting ready to put on a Thai food fair at the annual convention. By this time Moira was fluid in the genre and getting beyond just making Pad Thai. She found it challenging yet relaxing, realizing that French and American cuisine were not enough for her repertoire, if she was going to make it to executive chef one day.

Two days after the convention the crew was to fly to Asia. As the evening wound down, everyone was unpacking the catering truck and tidying up the kitchen for the night crew.

Standing outside the cellar, enjoying the cool of the evening—out of nowhere, Moira found herself being verbally attacked by Nancy.

"You know it is your fault, right?"

Peering at the truck, she noticed that tears were streaming down Mali's face as she once again argued with the Matriarch. Moira was feeling a pang that she did not yet understand.

"You know she is not coming back, is not coming back to America—part of the trip is to take her home. She is in love with you, everyone thinks you are having an affair, it is a great sin to her people, and they are punishing her by making her go home."

"That's ridiculous. But…"

"When you brought her to the managers' meal, everyone knew."

Almost knocking the babbling gossip down, Moira dashed to the truck, grabbed the weeping girl's hand, and ran her into the chilly walk-in refrigerator.

She finally took a real look, stared, at the beautiful girl, the girl who would do anything to please her, who had been begging her but did not have the words, did not even know how to say gay… A passionate little double of her: her Asian doppelganger.

Moira almost started to hyperventilate.

"*Pom ben* GAY?"

"Yes, GAY, GAY, love you…gay…"

Moira regained her breath and kissed the Asian girl's plum collared mouth. The kiss was returned fervently as they stroked each other's hair and pulled each other closer than possible. They exchanged air as if not to do so was to die. Moira closed her eyes and saw the moon and the stars, blue skies, the ocean—she was almost tripping. Maybe she was. But it was the realest thing to ever happen to her.

Pom ben gay!!! The walk-in felt like it was 80 degrees; the girls looked at each other and giggled hysterically. They floated out of the walk-in, hand-in-hand and marched up to the Matriarch. The whole of the staff stood back with awed respect. Even Nancy was silent.

"Mali does not want to go home!" Moira stated with steady conviction. "We are each other's—we will stay together." The Matriarch looked defeated: she knew she had lost, and quietly handed Moira Mali's work visa.

Moira's head was racing suddenly with thoughts of the house they would buy… not in Center City—too expensive—Germantown… they would make love and food and open their own Thai restaurant, the world was new. She saw her future and she liked it.

11:55

by

Denise Warner

After 25 years in South Florida, Denise now resides in South London, after marrying her wife, Jemma in 2010. She then threw herself into the international LGBT community, bringing her internet talk radio show from <u>MyLesbianRadio.com</u> to a new UK audience and making appearances and announcing acts at both The Go-Go Festival 2011 in Kent and The L-Fest in Shrewsbury (2011-2013). Denise continues to showcase her writing by writing the show content, and doing most of the cover interviews for the popular 'SHE Magazine' -a leading source for women -15 years strong in South FL (<u>www.shemag.com</u>). She also contributes to 'The Advocate' and 'Shewired.' Her interviews have included Melissa Etheridge, Wanda Sykes, Chely Wright, Joan Jett, Taylor Dayne, Margaret Cho, Fran Drescher, Sasha Alexander, Carmen Electra, Christina Aguliera, Jessica Clarke, the cast of 'Lip Service', Melissa Ferrick and Lucy Lawless.

I hate rushing. It makes me feel like I don't have my shit together. This isn't "oh my God, I'm late to pick up the kids again" late. This is different. The kids are with my mother tonight, and my wife is on her way home from work, as am I. Don't go thinking I'm competitive or anything, I just like getting home first, especially on a Friday night, because it's my night to cook—or, as I like to call it, "pick up sushi night". There's still a lot that goes into it, like opening the wine, setting the table, taking my shower, making sure the apartment is cleaned up—or at least being sure the kids' toys are put away. Listen, 8 years together and 2 kids later, "lesbian mommy date night" is not as common as it used to be. We both work for a snooty interior decorator named Lynda Hanes. My wife, Jill, is Lynda's long-time assistant, and I'm a painter. Once they secure the client and ridiculously overcharge them for decorating their places, I go to work with my team and get to the painting part. Most of the clients are rich, egotistical New Yorkers, like you would see on a "Real Housewives" show, which is fine, because I normally don't have too much interaction with them anyway. They adore my wife, with her British background and accent and her professional air. On the few occasions I have been at a job with my wife and a client, they have seemed to actually be under a spell, taking every piece of advice or suggestion as if it were coming from Queen Elizabeth herself. I love days when we cross paths at work. I think because it's a bit of a turn-on. No one would ever suspect us of doing the nasty later that night, the tightly wound British babe and the Italian-American former semi-pro softball player from upstate New York. Brings a smirk to my face every time. To look at my wife, you would never know she's a lesbian, with her Manhattan skirts, heels, long, perfectly-highlighted hair, well-manicured hands, and the latest designer handbag. To look at me, well...

you'd have a pretty good idea. You might not bet the entire farm on it, but probably a chicken or two. I'm not an "Albert Nobbs" or even a k.d. Lang type. I'd go as far as to say I'm a bit more feminine—along the lines of primetime TV's feisty female cop roles: a Jane Rizzoli, dipped in a Christine Cagney way. Plus, because I'm more of a project supervisor, I'm not dressed in sloppy overalls, spackle-splattered t-shirts and a tattered baseball cap anymore. Now, I'm all "khakis and cute boots", so I'm a little less obvious. It's been a typical work day for me, though I still had to stop off and pick up a key to another client's place for a job that was starting Monday morning. I didn't mind, actually, since it was in the building right next door to ours. I called my wife as I approached the lobby of the building.

"Hey, I'm at Ms Astley's building. I just have to pick up the key, right?" She giggled a little bit, which is most unusual for her (before 6pm).

"That's right. Did Lynda tell you anything about Ms Astley, by chance?" I stopped in my tracks.

"No. Why?" Being British, it seems almost instinctive for her to lower her voice if she's going to say anything remotely sexual, and I could sense it just about every time.

"She writes a sex advice blog," my wife said in a hushed tone. Now, it was my turn to chuckle.

"What, like Carrie Bradshaw?"

"Uh, no, for the Hustler Magazine triple X online site." I felt my one eyebrow jump.

"That's hard-core!" I snorted a laugh.

"Come in, come in," Ms Astley says, cheerfully, holding her yappy, tiny dog to her chest. I smile at the dog, wondering how stupid it must feel in that leopard-print tutu. At a glance, I can't imagine why she's having any painting done—the place is gorgeous—but leave it to Lynda to convince her it's needed.

Ms Astley looks like a tennis instructor with her tall, thin but muscular frame, blonde ponytail, all bouncy and spray-tanned. She's wearing heels that clickity-clack on the hardwood floors.

"I had a spare key made, and now I don't know what I did with it. Do you have a minute? I won't be long. Lynda and Jill told me how wonderful you are." Her voice trails as she makes her way down the hall, into another room. I prop myself against the arm of a magnificent sprawling sofa. It separates the kitchen area from the living room. As I gazed around, out of the corner of my eye, I could see Ms Astley's laptop open. I do a double take when I noticed there are tits, dicks, and ass all over the screen. Whoa! My brain immediately ordered my eyes, "Look away!" When I did, I was staring out the living room window, at my own apartment building. After taking a few steps closer to it, I realised that I could see my own kitchen window.

"So, sweetie, you'll be here on Monday?" Ms Astley called out as she rummaged. I couldn't pull my gaze from the window, I could clearly see right into our kitchen! My daughter's finger paint pictures on the refrigerator door, the lemon dish soap by the sink. That's our kitchen. Simultaneously thinking "Holy crap!" and "I left the milk out", I almost forgot to answer Ms Astley.

"Yep, Monday morning!" I could hear my voice, and it sounded like I was cheating on a test. What the hell?

"Excellent. I'll be gone for a few days. I'm going to an erotica convention on Saturday, and won't be back until mid-week. I'm so glad to be getting the guest rooms painted. Lynda and I go way back—old friends since the 80s: big hair, bad eyeliner, tons of blow."

I laugh out loud, shifting my attention to the general direction of Ms Astley's voice.

"The good old days," I say.

"Found them!" she says, re-entering, dangling the keys. The tiny dog stays at her ankles, nervously, as if someone might steal her.

"Oh, great! Your place is beautiful. This sofa ... it's just amazing," I say, taking the keys from her hand. She smiles warmly.

"Well, thank you. Lynda helped me pick it out a few years ago," she says, touching the fabric. "So, if I remember correctly, Lynda tells me that you and Jill are married?" I feel that awkward rush of blood to my cheeks that still tends to happen when I'm outside of a lesbian bar and the topic of sexuality comes up.

"Yep. Eight years. Two kids. Happy, happy..." my voice just drops off.

"That's wonderful!" Ms Astley says, with that Crest Whitestrips-white smile.

"Yeah. It really is... and... well... it's date night tonight. My mother is babysitting, and I... um... should really get going." Oh, for Christ's sake—why am I telling her this?! I hold up the keys in a clumsy attempt to remind her of the reason why I'm standing there in the first place.

"How lovely! After eight years, and two kids, having a 'date night' is fabulous! I get letters that address that very same idea every day! I tell people all the time in my column, 'you have to make time for yourselves because life gets in the way!' Right?"

"So, true, yes! Exactly!" I feel myself blushing, as if I'm talking to the school nurse about tampons. "Well... I'm off..." I do that retarded stutter step, not knowing if she's going first or if I should walk past her. She lets me pass, and follows me to the door. She opens the door for me and casually looks towards the living room window.

"Lynda says you live nearby?"

"I do, just across the way," I say, being as vague as possible. Does she know? Should I say anything?

"That's great," she says, "we should all do lunch one day." Why am I inching down the hall like a... tiny dog in a tutu?

"Yes! Great! Thanks! Okay..." Ms Astley steps a bit further into the hall and, with a devilish grin, looks me dead in the eye, and says,

"You show that wife of yours a good time tonight."

By the time Jill walks in, I've got my act together. The milk has been thrown out, the kids' toys are put away, the table is set, the wine is uncorked, I'm showered, dressed comfortably, our sushi is set out and ready at the intimate little kitchen table, with a single candle lit. Yes, I can now see Ms Astley's living room, though her blinds are drawn a bit. It was distracting for the first 15 minutes that I was home, because I kept checking angles to see what I thought she may be able to see and vice-versa. I do find myself glancing over there, as if to see if anything has changed. Jill never takes long to get comfy. She returns from the bedroom in drawstring pants and a thin t-shirt. I love the transition from business savvy to perfect girl-next-door that the weekend brings. She pours our wine, and sits at the table. By this time, the sun is setting, as evening rolls into night.

"So, what did you think of Ms Astley? Quite a character, isn't she?" I grin and nod, yet find myself instantly looking just past Jill out the window. I catch a glimpse of what appears to be skin. Flesh. Ass, to be exact. I take a sip of wine, not wanting to stare. With my next casual glance, I can more than make out that Ms Astley is totally nude. She's bent over the arm of her sofa, and a young naked man is behind her.

"More wine?" I ask Jill, nearly filling her glass to the rim. As Jill talks about picking up the kids tomorrow, I can feel myself getting warmer. The wine? Ms Astley getting banged from behind? The fact that it's been over a month since Jill and I had more than a make-out session and some over-the-shirt squeezes? I take a sip of wine, and move closer to kiss her. Leading Jill to our bed, date night turns into the predictable yet satisfying sex we've grown accustomed to. Until a bit later. Jill throws on her crumpled clothes from the bedroom floor, making her way to the fridge for a bottle of water. I follow her, thinking I'll do the dishes even though it's late. I can't help but look across the way. Wow. Naked Ms Astley, on the sofa still, now lowering herself onto her lover's lap as his hands grip her waist. Jill notices me staring,

"What?" She peers out, too and suddenly gasps.

"Is that Ms…?!"

"Shhh…" I whisper in her ear as we both watch as Ms Astley grinds into him. The lighted digits from our microwave cast a bluish glow in the kitchen as we stare out the window. 11:55PM. Then, without words, Jill and I lock into a tongue twirling kiss as I press her against the sink countertop. It's one of those kisses that starts off sensual, gets deeper, and then there's no denying where it's headed. I turn her around; running my hands under her shirt, cupping and massaging her breasts. Her head tilts back as I kiss her neck hotly, undoing the drawstring on her pants.

I hear her breathing getting rapid. My hand slips between her legs and her hips respond. The actual surprise of this moment, loaded with the passion that's always there but rarely gets acted upon anymore, creates an unbridled heat. Slow and gentle isn't even an option. Jill grinds against my hand, my breasts pressed against her back. I can feel own her hand cover mine, adding to both my and her sensation. In a flash, I look up and see Ms Astley from the window. She gives me that devilish grin again, accompanied by a wink this time, from across the way. Now, it was my turn to smile back as I fucked my wife against the kitchen sink.

SHINJUKU NIGHTSHIFT

by

Jade du Preez

Jade du Preez is a writer based in Auckland, New Zealand, currently working towards completion of her first novel, 'The Prince Who Would Not Be King'. With a day-job in graphics, after-hours are divided between the painting studio and a bomb-proof laptop. Her latest project is a collaborative LGBT-themed zine 'Transitory Spaces' featuring slice of life stories in a graphical form.

I kick around the corners that the shadows seep from. It's been a week now since Mr Tanaka's finger was cut off. Happened on this same street. Same time, I guess—the time of evening that colour disappears. Puddled water could be ink, could be blood. I heard he was 40-ish, tall-ish, quiet-ish. It's not the kind of news printed on the back of the Asahi Daily, more the kind of story that gets laced together from snatches of smoke-break conversation. I can't say who I'd heard it from—maybe a lady boy? Maybe he'd overheard from a delivery guy talking to the house mama.

I don't suppose you'd think it right to call him "lady boy". After all, what might he call me?

Gender-bender?

Cocktail-vendor?

Shoulder-lender, happy-ender?

Chest-binding, suit-wearing general pretender?

Well hey, who knows? Perhaps it was in the news? If I could see you again, I would ask. I'm sure you'd know. Do academics of classical history keep an eye out for history in the making?

You probably should.

You probably don't.

In my experience it's academics, you with the most structured of learning, who come out with the strangest trivia. This one client, a med student—she told me it was possible to feel every part of your body through the feet. Seriously! Later we experimented with a kind of perverted podiatry. We attempted to map out the sensory location of vital organs. Our success was, at best, limited. In the end she opted for a more direct approach. She left cash; scrolled like a diploma, fastened with her hair-tie. I don't suppose you'd want to know about that.

I'm at the start of my workday, handing out packaged tissues to commuters at the end of their work day. It's hard to catch the gaze of most. I wonder: if things had started differently, would you have looked up? Would you have refused? I can't dwell on it now; I have a small stash to get through. On each package is printed:

The Beautiful Boys of Club Ganymede Welcome You!

12-31-2 Shinjuku-sanchōme

Cocktails. Karaoke. Cool Hosts for every taste.

¥2000 Entry. Women only.

A man (not helpful) takes a tissue pack, barely stopping to mumble "thank you". He's tall, maybe 40, but appears to have a full set of digits. I wonder about Mr Tanaka, now only able to count to 4 and a half on one hand. Does he miss his baby finger? It's the baby finger most commonly referred to in the gossip. The story, as I understand it, is that he wanted to leave the Yakuza, just didn't feel cut out for mafia life anymore, or maybe he wanted to be a baker, or got married, had a kid—who knows? As a show of respect and to buy his way out he sacrificed his finger. Common practice. I fancy it was done with a heavy cleaver, a "Ki-ya!", and all while maintaining a stony expression. I can imagine the mafia boss, his cronies, and especially the finger donor, all stoic in the face of ritual. Still, I bet he misses his finger.

I fell in love with a finger once. A fingernail, really—it was even better in its full set. They were painted deep purple, entirely without an irregular edge. The enamel was heavy, rounded, perfect as the skin of a fresh aubergine. One such fingernail had tapped on the surface of the bar to get my attention.

"You," its owner had said. "Our table would like to meet you."

It was marvellous being met with such a fine, film-noir set of nails. So unblemished, so glossy! I brought over a tray of champagne flutes and instructed my colleague to follow with a bottle of our finest.

It's all part of it, being a host, being the stand-in for a clueless boyfriend or absent husband. For the purposes of my craft, I have learnt to fall in love with a great many aspects of very many women. I have fallen in love with arched eyebrows and asymmetrical fringes and delicate earlobes. With long necks and anxious shoulders and affected wrists. With deep laughter and high trills and unusual phraseology.

And you.

And when it came to you, given that you weren't a real client, nor even looking to be, I found I couldn't break you down into component parts. When I took in the view of your face, flashing white, then orange, lime, violet, blue, in the frenetic lighting of the club, I got stuck. I was flooded with a ridiculous, joyful sense of familiarity. No, we hadn't met, but it was that same feeling, the kind when you go to the train station, look out into the crowd, and find the face of a friend. You feel the pull of their connection to you and inverse repulsion to others. You find them completely alien, totally out of place, in such a field of strangers. Do you understand?

Now the street is filling in with darkness. I've given out most of the tissues. I'm mainly catching women on their way to Yotsuya station. They'll be heading home, thinking about yellow-lit rooms with microwave beeps and the opening music of their favourite soap operas. Perhaps they'd think it over and be back sometime. It's not that business is slow. Certainly, the mark-up on drinks allows for a constant intake of new "boys". It has been five years. I don't feel new anymore.

"You're like a Disney prince," you'd once said. "Perfectly dressed, elegantly moving and not a testicle to speak of."

I had been stumped. What a foreign thing to come out of such a familiar mouth as yours!

"Is there much to speak of when it comes to testicles?" I'd answered.

"Maybe more to say of testicles than of elegance."

"Each to her own," I'd said.

"You don't understand."

I didn't. I wonder if I'm starting to.

Remember when I visited you at that university cafeteria? The one where the seats are all busted leather and they huff and catch you like a baseball mitt? You'd been immune to the embrace of the furniture, perching on the edge, legs crossed at the knee. You wouldn't put down your saucer. It was held perfectly still in one hand, while you lifted and replaced your teacup with the other. Everything looked practised, ceremonial, calm. I'd once seen a woman at a shrine making similar movements. In prayer she'd held strips of paper between two fingers, raised them to her forehead, paused, murmured and flicked them into a fire. I didn't stay to ask what they were for. I pretended they were for me.

"So, Club Ganymede," you'd said. "Ganymede, the favourite of Zeus. The original androgyne."

"I don't know the story," I'd said.

"You should," you'd said.

And you told me about the shepherd-turned-cup-bearer and the dubious nature of consent involved in love between Gods and mortals. You said that while Troy mourned below, the King of the

Gods held this beautiful boy up to the sun and was more dazzled by the boy. It seemed that this virtue alone, his lovely countenance, was the deciding factor in their unusual arrangement. I asked whether this God would just get bored. You said no. I asked whether this God had a wife. You said he did, but that it was a detail of little consequence.

I instantly accepted all of these things to be true.

You told me about your husband, that you loved his shoulders, specifically the distance between them. You loved that his body was so flat and his spine so long, that when he wore a white shirt he took on the aspect of a ship's sail. That was before you began taking an interest in playing with the buttons on my shirt. That was before you took to rolling the top button between thumb and forefinger, easing it out of its buttonhole. Then the next, then the next. You placed great value in symmetry. You would stroke your palms down either side of my neck, slide them away from each other until the shirt, too small for a sail, would slip to the floor. You would reach around and release the clasp from between my shoulder blades and pass your hand around to the centre of my chest and slowly unwind the binding bandage. Around and around pausing at precisely the same points the way a pirouetting ballerina watches her mark.

Your finger nails left their trace in lines that merged then ran parallel down my spine. A Y or an X, always a symbol of symmetry.

Sailing ship? When I met him I thought your husband looked a little nerdy. Not in the academic way, more the secretive fan-boy type. The kind with a long-burning shame, a just-hidden animosity. I don't mean it in a cruel way, it's just the feeling I got. He didn't know enough to dislike me for any other reason, did he?

Was he a Disney Prince for you? I never asked. I don't imagine it. I don't suppose the Classics have much to do with Disney and you don't go in for simple stories, do you? Balance, you'd said, balance was what kept flavours freshest, music more moving, encounters more rewarding. I'd said I wasn't interested in being the counterpoint to your husband, a submarine to his sailboat. You laughed, said you couldn't imagine Atlantis would make for a suitable habitat. Not for me.

I suppose I just existed in your afternoons. I existed when my work hadn't started and your lectures weren't of interest. I suspected that you missed more than you should, but what did I know about university? Other than you thought I'd like it there. Other than you wished we'd met there instead, or earlier. In the afternoons in your apartment we used to imagine how we might have taken to each other having met in high-school, junior school, kindergarten. In every story we fell in love. But those were just stories.

"I suppose you'll have to go," you said last time.

I already knew you didn't mean temporarily.

"Why?"

"Because I can't take you in the measure you can provide."

I was stung. Were we back to talking of testicles and perfection?

"What does that mean?" I'd said.

"Your job," you'd said. "It's so limited, I don't know if you mean…?" You gripped the sheets. All your clever words fell away.

"Without this job I can't survive. Not in this city."

"Okay," you said.

"Without your marriage, how would you study?"

"Okay."

All that balance off kilter. Or perhaps it was "okay" for you. You turned away as I left. I was robbed of the sight of that strangely familiar face before I even closed the door. Who am I to change? Who are you to ask me?

Truthfully, it wasn't a bad idea. I could go on with my version of Ganymede, and you could go on with yours. It would be fine. So many books and so many clients. It would be fine.

Keep me in your sun.

I have one packet of tissues left. I smile, hold them out to a woman in a pink coat. She ducks her head and walks faster. Another, older woman walks past and looks coldly at me. I'm never sure of how much people guess at what I do. There are many men. I see one approaching, he coughs into his hand and it's bandaged! A bright, white bandage makes a fat, undeniably shorter stump of the small finger on his left hand. He pauses in front of me, nods, says thanks, and takes the last package from me.

He'll be going from his hypothetical bakery that smells of European breakfasts and melted chocolate and where great sacks of flour and sugar stand like guards. He'll be heading home to his theoretical wife, who is relaxing into believing that her husband is gentle, kind and measured. He'll be picking up his potential child, a boy, who grins the way he once did, who doesn't know him as anything other than "Dad". I think he was smiling, that Mr Tanaka. What's a little finger in this world?

I have no advertisements left. In the darkness, the wind seems to go through me. I should head back. It's a short walk east to the Club. It's a shorter walk north to the subway station. There are only three stops to your apartment. You haven't heard this story about Mr Tanaka.

THE AFFAIR

by

Mel King

Inspired by history and dark fantasy, Mel has been writing for some years now and has studied creative writing at several levels. She would like to go on to become a full novelist, if all the ideas would stop vying for attention.

Birmingham, 2010

Seven thirty and she's still not here. I watch the face of my timepiece intensely, counting the seconds and minutes past the hour when we were supposed to meet. The coffee set out for her is cold; mine, empty. I wish I could smoke in here.

Sitting back in my badly-padded booth and looking over my mirrored sunglasses, I scan the faces of the other diners. An old couple holding hands over their weak teas, knowing that one of them is dying inside from a medical "complication"; a young man and his guide dog, groping for the last bite of his cake, only to find that the waitress already took it away and spat in his coffee; a woman in a moth-eaten fur coat, crying into her latte, her lost lover a conman; and finally the waitress, stood behind the counter popping gum with her mouth wide open. Her mind is empty. I want to shove something in the gaping hole.

Twenty to eight, I almost get up to leave, but it is raining outside. Good. Let the bitch get wet.

I resume watching the clock, wishing I had a book, paper, anything. I note that the clock above the bimbo waitress is exactly fifty seconds behind mine. I wonder why I'm still here, then remember what she's going to do to me if I leave. I signal to the waitress to come over, but she ignores me. She is busy flipping through some celebrity magazine, still popping gum. I want it to stick her mouth closed.

The door opens, and I find my world get lighter.

At exactly quarter to eight, Miss Kinnock enters the dreary café and shakes out her soaked umbrella. Her hair had become tangled in the wind and she runs her hands through it attempting to straighten the frizz. I like the frizz. She tries not to smile as she approaches me and sits down opposite.

I don't look up from my watch, so Miss Kinnock looks for the waitress.

"Don't," I tell her.

Miss Kinnock leans in.

"What?"

"No coffee. Drink the one I got for you."

She looks down at the small cup. The dark liquid had spilled into the saucer a little, making it look as if it had been crying.

"Francesca..." she starts, but I look up over my sunglasses, letting her see my eyes.

"Do it."

Slowly, she brings the cup to her lips. I watch, keeping her eyes locked with mine, betraying nothing.

The coffee is tepid and bitter. I know she would like sugar to take the edge off, but I won't let her. She deserves this. Closing her eyes, she begins to drink the fouled liquid, taking it in gulps just to get rid of it faster.

Finishing, she places the cup down and tries not to gag. Looking down, I note the time.

"Ten to eight."

"I couldn't get away earlier."

"Try harder."

"You know He doesn't like it if we leave early."

"He isn't on my time."

Miss Kinnock sighs and leans back.

"Well, I'm here now."

I smile for the first time, reaching out to her.

"Yes you are."

We giggle together, like we're sixteen, holding hands, allowing our fingertips to touch and stroke one another. There are small sparks in the dim light.

She sighs, and licks her lips, pulling away from me.

"It's so nice to see you again."

I grin, flashing my teeth. She shudders.

"Then we shouldn't waste time. Shall we?"

I stand and help her up, deliberately pressing my warm body into her cool one. She laughs and grabs my neck, pulling me into a kiss. She always keeps her mouth closed. The tease.

Clicking my fingers, I ignore the stares of the café's patrons as we leave for the damp street. Let them think what they want, I am with her.

As the door closes, the waitress begins to choke on her gum.

The Silver City, the year of the birth.

The door was painfully white, reflecting the light of thousands of beings committed to "the cause". It made my skin want to peel and my eyes melt from their sockets. I squinted instead.

I was escorting some pumped up diplomat from the Seventh Circle on a mission to discuss some mortal who has just been born to be a great prophet or something. Apparently our lot had a temptation contract out, and needed to squeeze out the final details. Boring, but I had no choice. I just did what I was told.

My diplomat knocked thirteen times, barely keeping in his tentacles. I guess the older you are, the harder it is to keep in your taint. This guy had it in spades. We waited for a heartbeat, and the door slowly opened inward by itself, making no sound. Creepy.

Beyond the door was a little less bright, but it still made me want to turn tail and run. It was all so… white. Purity distilled into a place. I noticed that our footprints left smudges on the floor's sheen. We were greeted by three of Them, wielding spears made of light and wings of purity itself. I wanted to pluck them, smug bastards.

Silently, they gestured at us, herding us along the walkway to a small building, where the vision was standing. I tried not to gawp. I failed. Just a little bit.

The vision had bigger wings than the others, folded neatly at her back. Her skin was radiance itself, framing ruby lips and eyes as blue as the sky. Her hair cascaded down her back like a river of gold. Unlike the guards, she was wearing a diaphanous robe, while they were naked. This one was a Muse, and I tried not to instantly fall in love. If I had a soul, it would have wept. She was holding a scroll, and wrote something with a quill before coming to meet us. I remember trying not to fidget in her presence. When faced with perfection, it's hard not to feel like an ant.

"I will state this: you are in Heaven, so obey the rules. No wandering, no talking to the residents and no..." she looked at me, "...sinning. That is all." I tried not to smile, instead coming out with a half smirk that danced across my face rudely, to which I got a raised eyebrow.

She opened the door for my charge, and he entered, followed by the guards. She closed the door right in my face before I could enter.

"Official personnel only."

"Pffft, whatever you say." I leant against the building. Where I touched it, there were sparks. It made my back itch.

We stood in silence for a while, and I tried to ignore her. I tried whistling, to which I got a glare. Tapping had the same effect.

She stood so straight, staring into nothing as she was patient. I hate patience. Finally, I fished the dark cigarettes out of my pocket and sparked up, taking the blue smoke into my body. Oh, yes. My lot created them a long time ago. As I exhaled, the smoke was snuffed out by the light. She looked at me like I just ate the forbidden fruit.

"You can't smoke up here."

"Why not? It's not like it smells."

"It's blasphemy."

I looked over at her out of the corner of my eye. She was deadly serious—even her wings were twitching. I smiled at her, licking my lips with a forked tongue. She shuddered.

"Have you ever tried it?"

She frowned again.

"Don't tempt me."

"It's what I do best, sweetness."

"I'm not your sweetness. Put it out."

Catching her gaze and looking directly into her, I licked my lips. She stared, transfixed, as I put the cigarette out on my tongue. She blinked twice and shuddered, forcing herself to look away.

"Stop that."

"Why?"

"It's not fair."

I laugh.

"None of this is fair, sweetness. That's the point."

2010

We stumble out into the wet streets, holding on to each other as if we might fall. The skies are still open, soaking us within minutes. We open our mouths to catch the water caressing our skin, laughing like we are innocent. She nuzzles into my neck as we walk, the umbrella forgotten. She knows I love it up here, and doesn't question. Her hair is frizzing up again, and I stroke the water through it. She is so beautiful.

The streets are empty at this time, the light from the lamp posts muted by the rain, casting flickering shadows into the alleys. At least today they are just shadows.

We are heading to the usual place. We meet like this every time we can get away from the boredom that is our eternal work, which is not often enough.

Keeping to the dark, hiding our bodies from any that would notice us, I lead her along. We are not the only ones to be up here. Many are on duty, and should they see us we would be in trouble, the kind of trouble that would leave her banished and me burning in some eternal pit like a mortal. No fucking way.

The light takes me by surprise as we turn the corner, the headlamps burning with a brighter light than they should. Red and blue lights on the top of the car give them away. Bloody Celestial Control—Angels in police uniforms. I pull Miss Kinnock along, running for the next street. The car behind me revs into action, following us.

I dash down a blind alley, hoping we can lose them if their car can't fit, only to come across a fence. I grab Miss Kinnock and push her above me so she can scale it and then follow myself. The car's light floods the alley just as we get over. Behind us, car doors open and a dog ruffs softly. Bugger.

I crush my companion to the wall, holding a hand over her mouth.

"Be still," I hiss.

We hold our breath as the policemen search the alley. I will myself to not sweat. Our eyes meet and hold, gripping each other as tense as our bodies. Time slows to a trickle. I hear the dog snuffling, the two cops looking for clues. The dog sniffs the fence once, then evidently finds something else to be interested in.

"There is nothing here," states one of them, his voice echoing in the silence.

"I am sure I saw something. Never mind. Let us go."

Thank the powers for dumb Angels! They leave the alley, and I hear the car moving away, leaving us in the blackness. I allow myself to relax, giving my partner a reassuring squeeze. Her mouth finds mine, hungry and scared.

Arsuf, the Holy Land, 1191

Weapons clashed and bodies screamed, all men thinking they were doing the will of Him, when they were doing the will of man. Souls sold themselves too easily here. Saladin and Richard, both men of the man upstairs, and each thinking the other one was in league with the Devil. Bodies littered the ground, some dark-skinned, some white, all martyrs to their cause. Idiots.

Both of Our forces were there too, dancing on the edges of Man's perception. Only those in great pain could see us, as their life ebbed away. We collected those who had sold themselves for power or money, just as they realised that it meant absolutely nothing when you were a dead man. The other side collected those that had the sense to pray for forgiveness, and those who were truly pious. Grunt work really, but I had been there to collect some I had personally tempted. I'm a stickler for the DIY principle when it comes to mortals.

I was leaning over some Templar who I had "encouraged" to pillage an innocent village, drawing out his essence into a jar, when I felt the presence of one of Them.

"I think you will find that he is mine."

Placing on the lid, I turned.

"Oh, yeah? What are you gonna... Oh. Hello."

I smiled despite myself—here was the Muse I had met so long ago and not been able to forget, resplendent in robes of white, her hands covered in the blood of the fallen. Gorgeous.

"Been here long?" I grinned.

"That soul belongs to Him." She pointed to the jar I was carrying. The red soul within pathetically thrashed against its prison.

"I don't think so. He is a cold blooded murderer. He's mine."

"Incorrect." She brought out a scroll and scanned what was written. "Sir Geoffrey Hampton; prayed for forgiveness to a priest last night."

"Killed seventy innocent villagers a week ago and didn't care," I countered.

"Unimportant. He pledged eternal chastity and flagellated himself for an hour, as is right." She raised an eyebrow at me.

"They were all women and children."

"Cried himself to sleep that very night and sought out confession the moment he rose."

"Shit."

Reaching out, she waited for me to put the jar in her hand. I looked at her delicately tapered fingers and sighed. Bitch.

"You can have him, but you have to tell me something first," I offered

She cocked her head, guarded.

"What?"

"Tell me your name." I grinned at her. To my surprise, she smiled back.

"Open the jar."

I did so, and the soul shot out. Flowing around her like water, it caught her hair, lifting her up in a cascade of light. She laughed lightly, her voice pulling me into a sigh. As it rippled, its colour changed slowly to purest white, before ascending.

She smiled happily and began to turn away.

"Hey! What about me?" I called.

She turned.

"What about you?"

"You owe me a name."

She laughed.

"I don't owe you anything, Demon. Names have power, you know that. You bargain with them."

"So?" I stated, petulantly. "You said you would. That's not fair."

She came to me then, laying a soft hand on my cheek. Where we touched, sparks of static made me shudder. Leaning into me, she whispered:

"None of this is fair. That is the point." She danced her fingers across my cheek and pulled away. I watched her go, wanting nothing more than to see her panting and grovelling at my feet.

"Hey!" I shouted, suddenly running after her. She stopped but didn't turn. "My name's Francesca!"

She turned, a wry smile on her face.

"You can call me Miss Kinnock."

2010

The hotel is small and off of the main street, the kind of place that sees many cheats through its doors. No questions asked. It has been such for several generations, and because it is run by a Lillim, it maintains a neutral policy on all things spiritual. Perfect.

We have barely picked up the keys and ascended the grimy stairs when she pushes her weight against me and takes my bottom lip into her mouth, biting down. I grunt my surprise and enjoyment, opening my mouth to her tongue.

She abruptly pulls away, nuzzling into my neck.

"I've been thinking of you since the Eighties," she breathes in my ear. Our mouths meet again, and I mumble my agreement into her, reaching past her to unlock the door.

Once inside, she's all down to business, ripping off my shades and pulling off my jacket before I can turn on the light. I laugh, pushing her onto the bed.

"Wait," I tell her. She smiles at me and leans back, throwing off her coat and pulling up her dress to reveal black stockings. I nod my approval, and she slips off the dress.

Black lace. I love this decade.

I turn the light on, banishing the darkness to the corners of the room. Everywhere is red velvet, patchy and badly cleaned. Pulling off my shirt and leather trousers, I go to her.

She bids me do everything: hot wax dripping onto naked flesh, her hands tied with rough rope; Miss Kinnock, panting like an animal, bidding me to do it again and again. Angels are so kinky. I love every moment stolen with her here, biting my ear, whispering blasphemies, making confessions to her Demon priest.

When she is spent, she lets me cradle her in my arms, crying softly. I tell her it will be okay, that one day we will no longer be on opposite sides.

I tell her I love her.

The Somme, 1916

Rivers of mud and blood, mortals shaking in the trenches, no longer able to hear anything but the noise. Boys died here, having lied to join the army, only to fall, full of fear and regret. A tasty snack for soul suckers. "You will be safe, just give me your soul"—not cool. I only take the evil.

Showers of mud and blood, the Allies running in their droves over the top into artillery fire and land mines. The officers desperate to take some ground, no matter the cost. The souls crying out for release. This place would be thick with them by the end, and the battle would continue raging with spirit soldiers, doomed forever, tied to the trenches.

I had been there with the tempters, basking in human suffering and collecting souls bargained for position and power. To be honest, there were slim pickings. The mortals just wanted out, and it wasn't in our jurisdiction. We don't grant wishes like that.

I'd had several soul jars full, and was picking my way along looking for some of the mad, when I heard crying that pulled at my energy. The sound of purity suffering. Finding my way, I came across the Muse, cradling some dead boy. His eyes were staring emptily, the horror clear on his youthful face. He was missing an arm, the stump ragged and dirty. He was lying in a puddle of his own blood, the flow creating patterns in the mud even then.

Her keening was making me ache, and I approached her slowly, just in case she took it out on me.

"Miss Kinnock?"

She looked up. Her face was still perfect, despite the tears. There was some recognition there, through her sorrowful haze. "It's me, Francesca."

She sniffed, stroking the boy's face.

"I know who you are, Demon."

"He's gone; you should let go now."

She looked down at him, smiling sadly.

"He was only fourteen. He had not told his parents he was going to war. No one will remember him. Such pain, he was in so much pain…" She trailed off, the tears flowing off of her shining cheek, landing on his grimy forehead.

"But you will remember," I whispered, placing a tentative hand on her shoulder.

She threw me off, standing and letting the body drop.

"How do you know, Demon? Eater of souls? You are here to steal the innocent! To doom them to eternal damnation! Damn you!" She pounded at me with her fists, taking her rage out on my body. I took the pain for a while, waiting for her to get it out of her system. When I'd let her beat me enough, I grabbed hold of her wrists and pulled her to me, holding her against my chest, letting her cry.

"I don't take the innocent. I can't, it's not fair," I whispered to her.

"Hell, this is Hell," Miss Kinnock sobbed. "There is no God here."

"Whoa, girl!" I said, looking into her eyes. "This is nothing to do with Him, upstairs or downstairs. This is man, pure and simple. Hey, don't cry. I hate it when Angels cry. It's not right." I patted her shoulder and fished for a handkerchief. She sniffed.

"God, I need a cigarette"

"Glad to oblige," I replied, fishing out my packet and offering her one, before taking one myself. We lit them with my battered lighter and sat as explosions set the ground shaking and mortal cries of pain filled the air. I watched her as she took the smoke in, coughing with every drag. At least it seemed to calm her somewhat.

She looked at me then, evaluating me.

"You aren't like most Demons, are you?"

"I'm a tempter, not a soul sucker. Those guys are just wrong."

"Why did you give me your true name?"

I smiled.

"I don't know. Maybe I thought I could trust you."

"But we are on opposite sides."

"Times are changing. Perhaps sides don't matter anymore. Besides, I couldn't help it."

"Help what?"

I looked into her eyes. She knew the answer.

2010

Sated, we return to the streets, contented and holding one another. The rain has stopped, and the streets have a sparkling sheen. We both know we might never see the other again, so are silent. No goodbyes, not for us.

Heading down the dead end alley, we ignore the drunken bum. He won't remember ever having seen us, and if he does—well, he is just a mad tramp. She hugs me one last time and we share a kiss, before she stands away from me and readies herself.

I stand back as the light begins to grow, and her wings emerge, resplendent in the dark alley, surrounded by rubbish. She waves to me once, before she heads upward. I put my shades back on before my retinas are burned through.

A flash and she is gone. I let my vision return to normal, then place twenty pounds in the tramp's tin. He mumbles his thanks, and I smile. He will die tonight of a heart attack, his clothes stolen by others of the streets. He will be discovered by a policeman tomorrow, naked and alone. At least he will die happy.

I begin to kick a can down the street, humming to myself. I'll tell her next time that her feathers have a streak of grey.

IT COMES NATURALLY

by

Ruth Moorman

Ruth lives in Indiana and blogs about life, love and being gay in the Midwestern US at onethirstyfish.blogspot.com. She follows her passion for writing, reading and graphic design, and has an incurable weakness for all things cute.

Left cheek. Right cheek. Forehead, nose, chin. Left cheek. Right cheek. Forehead, nose, chin. Her skin is warm as I kiss her face gently in the systematic pattern. Left cheek. Right cheek. Forehead, nose, chin. Her eyelashes flutter. She is so close. Left cheek. Right cheek. Forehead, nose, chin. Left cheek. Right cheek. Forehead, nose...

I don't make it to her chin this time. I find her lips instead.

She wasn't in her dorm room. Or the cafeteria. Or the library. Or on the lawn in the setting sun. Or by the lake. She was gone. I'd missed my chance. Hot tears sprung to my eyes. How could this have happened? How could our friendship crumble after one stupid mistake? It was just a kiss.

But I knew that was a lie. I knew it was more than a kiss. And obviously she knew it too.

I met Laurie on my first day of my second semester of college in our "Fundamentals of Genetics" course. I awoke that morning with a start at 8:20 a.m., with that sick feeling when you realise you've overslept. I raced to my 8:00 a.m. class, kicking myself that I was late on my very first day. As I opened the classroom door my heart was pounding; I tripped over my untied shoes, sent the door slamming into the wall with a loud bang and startled the entire class—even causing one of the girls to let out a high-pitched squeal. The room went quiet and the professor looked up at me, unamused.

"Your name?" he asked.

"Tara Abrams," I answered, mortified. He found my name on the roster. My face was beet red as I scanned the room for an empty seat. I became very conscious of the fact I was dishevelled with my hair falling out of a ponytail and flying off in all directions, my shoes untied and my big comfy hoodie slouching down on one side. And then I saw her: she was smiling at me with a bemused expression. The seat next to her was open so I hurried over and sat down.

When the professor began talking again, she leaned over, her long, straight hair falling in front of her face a little. Her eyes sparkled mischievously as she whispered,

"Hey, I'm Laurie. It's Tara, right? As in Tara *the Terror*?"

"What?" I asked, caught off guard by this strange girl talking to me. She was pretty—lightly freckled skin and light brown hair—but no makeup. She wore a simple sweater and jeans, but she looked fresh and bright—definitely not like someone who'd just jumped out of bed.

"You scared us all half to death, slamming the door like that." She tipped her head toward the front of the room. "He had already put most of us to sleep in the first ten minutes with his lecture."

The professor had resumed his talk about the diagrams projected on the screen. It was true, quite a few students were already drifting off again to the dull sound of his voice.

I grinned, picturing what a scene it must have made in the dark sleepy classroom when I fell in the door.

"I do always strive to make a grand entrance," I whispered back. She snorted a laugh, causing a few people to glance over at us.

Laurie burst into my galaxy like a new star being born. One day, there was darkness, and the next day, there she was—glowing bright and pulling me into her orbit. I'd see her from a distance, walking across campus. I'd notice her ahead of me in the cafeteria line, laughing with her friends. If she saw me, she'd smile. It made my heart flip over. She'd sneak up on me in the library and whisper *"Tara the Terror!"* to make me jump, and I'd punch her in the shoulder.

Our transition from strangers to friends was effortless. We bonded over our love of science. She loved biology and ecology—anything to do with life and growth and things being made new and the interactions between creatures and the earth. Laurie was the only girl I knew who wouldn't freak out when she saw a bug. She would grab a jar and trap the poor thing in order study it closely, throwing little bits of grass and dirt in there to "create an environment" for it. I would laugh at her, but she didn't care. When she'd learn all there is to know about the thing, she'd "release it back into the wild". Occasionally the creature would die in captivity and she would have a very small funeral for it, burying it in the earth, marking the spot with a twig. In this way she was so innocent, almost like a child in the way she viewed the world around her—she found it endlessly fascinating.

I, on the other hand, appreciated the mechanics and systems of the scientific world: the mathematical side of the laws of physics and the interactions of elements on a chemical level. These things were certain. They were calculable. There were forces and reactions and equations. You could form a hypothesis and either prove or disprove it to find a truth. I craved absolute truths and solutions to problems.

Classes like Fundamentals of Genetics didn't spark my interest. There were too many unknowns, and too many uncontrollable variables. It was lucky I had Laurie in that class with me. She would text me in the evening, eager to go check on her "baby makers", the fruit flies we were observing and breeding for the lab portion of the class. We'd go over to the 24-hour science building late at night, smuggling in snacks and coffee, and set up camp in the lab where all the fruit flies lived in their hundreds of tiny vials. Laurie loved to watch them flitting around in their miniature communities. Being born. Mating. Dying. Living out their short lives, proportional to their tiny speck-sized bodies.

One night we were in the lab, working quietly on some homework, when I happened to glance over and see Laurie watching me.

She took advantage of my attention to break the silence.

"Tara, have you ever dated anyone?"

We had talked in passing about her ex-boyfriend, Tom, from high school. They had broken up when she left for college. Somehow, I had avoided the question for myself. Until now.

"Um, not really, no," I admitted to her.

"Really? That's crazy!" she said in disbelief. "You're so gorgeous and exotic with those dark eyes and dark hair... I can't believe no guy has snatched that up." She was teasing.

I was one-quarter Indian. My grandmother had immigrated to the U.S. from India after she had met my grandfather and fallen in love. I had her light mocha skin, thick curly hair and hourglass figure.

I contemplated this for a moment.

"It's not that I haven't come across a few potential snatchers," I grinned at her, "I just managed to remain... un-snatched and unattached."

She looked at me with those piercing green eyes for a moment. My face got hot. I decided to take a plunge.

"Laurie, can I tell you something?" I asked.

"Of course you can."

"And you won't... make fun of me?"

"Well, that depends. But I'll do my best not to."

I took a deep breath.

"I... well, I've... I've never kissed anyone."

It was something I avoided telling anyone. I was 19, everyone my age seemed to have already kissed plenty of people. What was wrong with *me*? When other girls asked about my first kiss or how many guys I'd made out with, I always played it off with a vague answer, something playful like "oh, *you know*..." with a wink, or an "I don't kiss and tell." But I trusted Laurie to not make fun.

"Tara, that's totally okay. That just means you're smarter than most girls by not wasting kisses on just any guy. You're waiting for the right one."

I nodded.

"Thanks." Relief washed over me.

She looked back down at her textbook and resumed her homework. I thought for a moment and then interrupted her.

"Laurie?"

"Yeah," she said, not looking up.

"How will I know—how will I know for sure it's the right one? And how will I know what to do and how to kiss?"

She looked at me across the lab table and rested her hand gently on my arm.

"Tara, trust me, you'll know. And you'll know what to do. This type of thing is built into us." She pointed to one of the fruit fly test tubes. "See? Even *they* know what to do. It comes naturally when the time is right."

She gave me a little wink and laughed.

I smiled and said, "If you say so."

Laurie had more experience than me, so she must know what she was talking about.

The semester flew by. As the weather turned from winter to slush, and from slush to spring, Laurie was always pulling me along to venture outside. We'd hike through the woods in search of little streams, we'd spend time just lying on the grass in the sun while we studied (she insisted that outdoors was truly the only place you could truly absorb science). My favourite was when we went out on the warmer nights and looked at the stars. Stars were my constants, and I found it comforting that I always knew where to find them. Absolute truths.

There was a small lake at the edge of campus, not far from the science building. Some nights, when we needed a break from studying, we'd go sit at the water's edge and listen to the bullfrogs and the crickets and the quiet little splashes of fish hunting for their food. I would whistle a tune into the dark. Laurie always loved it when I did that; she couldn't whistle. She said it let the little creatures around the pond know that we were here, and that we were friendly—just singing our song as a greeting.

This is where we were a few nights before the end of the semester. I didn't want it to end. In a week we'd both be far away from here, far away from each other. I sighed as I lay back on the grass in the dark. I filled my lungs and whistled a slow, melancholy tune into the night.

"That's a new one," Laurie said. "It sounds kind of... sad. But it's beautiful."

"I'm letting all of them know we're leaving soon," I answered, as though the bullfrogs might be concerned that we'd be gone for a few months.

She was quiet.

"Tara?"

I loved it when she said my name.

"Yeah"

"You're, well... I don't want to lose you over the summer. I know we'll be far apart, but you won't forget about me, right?"

As if that were possible.

"Of course we'll keep in touch. It's just a few months anyway—we'll be back here in no time at all."

"Okay, good. I'd like that."

"Me too, Laurie."

"Tara?"

"Yeah"

"You're my best friend."

"I know," I said, my heart swelling with joy. The huge cheesy grin on my face was hidden in the dark.

I started whistling again. The tune happier this time.

Finals week stormed in with hours full of sleep-deprivation—lots of late night quests for caffeine, cramming our brains with every last bit of information that would fit without shoving something else out the other side.

The night before our Genetics final I had resigned myself to "letting the chips fall".

"If I don't know it by now, then I'm not going to!" I explained to Laurie, exasperated as she quizzed me on terms. She tried to stifle a yawn.

"Fine," she said, "but I still want to study. So if you're done, then go get me some coffee."

"It's 2:30 a.m. already, are you sure?"

"Please please, pretty please?" she begged.

When I got back with the coffee from the 24-hour gas station, Laurie had fallen asleep with her textbook open on her chest. I studied her for a moment. Her hair was splayed on the pillow. Her T-shirt was bunched up, exposing the smooth skin of her stomach. Her lips were parted as she breathed steadily. Every cell in my body was pulled towards her.

I carefully lifted up her textbook and placed it on her nightstand along with her coffee. I took off my shoes, flipped off the switch on the light and crawled into bed next to her. I was startled when she spoke, I must have woken her.

"What time is it?" she asked sleepily.

"Shhh, it's three, let's go back to sleep," I soothed her.

She pulled me in close, her hand on my waist. My hips were almost touching her hips, my arm draped over her. I felt the warm skin of her abdomen. Our noses were inches apart as we lay face to face on her pillow. I could see her outline, but it was too dark to see her eyes.

"I need to study more," she protested half-heartedly.

I chuckled.

"You're going to do great, you know these chapters backwards and forwards."

Her breath was warm on my face. I felt her sigh.

It struck me suddenly how incredibly precious this girl was to me. My sweet, beautiful friend; she had found a way into my heart and it almost hurt how much I cared for her.

I lifted my head and kissed her cheek. Her left cheek, right cheek. Her forehead, her nose… and then her chin. She lay perfectly still. I repeated the pattern of kisses. Left cheek, right cheek. Forehead, nose, chin. The room was so quiet, I could hear my heart beating, I could feel her eyelashes flutter against my chin. Left cheek, right cheek. Forehead, nose, chin. I kissed her face slowly and gently. Lingering long enough to feel the heat of her skin on my lips.

I'll never know exactly what possessed me in that moment—the moment that changed everything. But on the next rotation of kisses, I stopped on the way from her nose to her chin and softly kissed her lips.

Lightning shot through my brain as a spark passed between us. My heart rate doubled and I felt like I was about to spontaneously combust.

Her lips were parted and she took in a quick breath. I felt her body tense next to me.

I couldn't stop myself, I kissed her lips again. The top lip, so soft. The bottom lip, full between my lips. I kissed them slowly and tentatively.

And then, it happened. The most strange, wonderful sensation. Laurie began to kiss me back. *She* kissed *me*. Her lips started moving against mine, her hand gripped my side, pulling me closer. I could feel the wet of the inside of her lips. We kissed again and again and again. I think my mind must have short-circuited at some point because I don't remember how long it went on. It felt like a blissful eternity; I didn't want it to stop. Our breathing was heavy but controlled. My body was on fire. We lay still and held each other so close. We didn't use any tongue. We didn't move an inch. I kissed her. She kissed me. And hours passed. The next thing I knew I woke up to the sound of the alarm—it was 7 a.m.—and Laurie dove over me to turn it off. She sat back and said,

"Let's get to class early and review for the test."

I failed the test.

If it had been a test about Laurie's lips and first kisses, I would have aced it, because that was all I could think about. I sat in the classroom, staring at the blank pages. *Did it really happen? Did*

Laurie not remember it? Did she not like it? What happens now? Fuckfuckfuckfuckfuck!

I could still remember the sensation of her smooth lips caressing mine. I could remember the way my body burned. I could remember the grip of her hand on my waist and the warmth of her so close to me. I could see the back of her head a few seats away. *Was she thinking about it too?*

I spent the day in agony. We both had full schedules for the day. I made eye contact with her as the herd of students exited the room, but then she was gone. I couldn't focus the rest of the day as I finished up my last exams. In every hall between classrooms, on every sidewalk between buildings, I looked for her. I willed her to appear, but she did not.

Straight after class I ran back to her dorm room. She couldn't avoid me forever. One way or another we were going to talk about this. I would take it all back, explain that I'd made a mistake—I'd do whatever it took to save our friendship. I would tell her I was exhausted from studying and had been mentally deranged. It was an accident. Several hours of accidental kissing…

I felt panic cinching in my chest. She'd never buy that. I wasn't going to lose her over this. It was just a kiss. I told myself that over and over—it was just a kiss. Nothing had to change.

She wasn't in her dorm room. Or the cafeteria. Or the library. Or on the lawn in the setting sun. Or by the lake. She was gone. I'd missed my chance. Hot tears sprung to my eyes. How could this have happened? How could our friendship crumble after one stupid mistake? It was just a kiss.

But I knew that was a lie. I knew it was more than a kiss. And obviously she knew it too.

A fly buzzed around my ear as I slumped to the ground next to the lake. The sun was setting. In the morning she'd be leaving. What if she left without saying goodbye? *Zzzzzzzz*—the fly hovered around my head and I lashed out and smacked it to the ground. His little wings twitched and then he was still. The sight of the dead little fly pushed me over the edge and I burst into sobs. I dug a small grave for him, just like Laurie would have done. *I ruin everything*, I cursed myself. Even tiny innocent creatures aren't safe around me. *Laurie, what have I done to us?*

I picked up a twig and carved in the dirt: "Here Lies Fly".

Fly. *The flies!*

I jumped to my feet and sprinted towards the science building. I had looked there already, but I forgot about the fruit fly lab—maybe Laurie was saying goodbye to them! I sprinted up the steps two-at-a-time and flung myself through the door.

Panting, I scanned the room.

It was empty. Even the fruit flies had been cleared out—all but a few vials had been disposed of. I remembered now that our professor had told us to go upstairs and chloroform our remaining flies after the final. I had completely forgotten. I walked over to the shelf labelled Abrams. Mine were gone.

"Tara the Terror," a voice said behind me.

My heart stopped and I turned around. Laurie was standing in the doorway holding several empty vials.

I opened my mouth to speak, but no words came out.

"I took them outside to release them into the wild," she said, holding up the vials. "It'd be so sad to kill them after they helped us out all semester."

She placed the tubes gently back on the shelf and walked over to me, her green eyes searching mine. Her brow furrowed as she took in my puffy red face and bloodshot eyes.

I finally stammered out, "I thought you had left." My voice came out all high-pitched and shaky.

"Tara, I've been looking for you all day…"

"Laurie, I'm so sorry, I ruined everything…"

This stopped her.

"I understand if you don't want to be friends anymore, but I'll do anything I can to save our friendship," I said resolutely, bracing myself for the consequences of my actions.

She looked confused.

"Tara."

"Yeah?"

"I love you."

"What? Like…?"

"Yes, like that."

"You… you aren't upset with me? I mean, you liked… you're okay with what happened…?"

I couldn't believe that's what she was really saying. But she had said it, said that she loved me. *Yes, like that.*

And if I still hadn't been sure, she further clarified by combing her fingers into my messy curly hair, pulling me in and kissing me long and hard. This time with tongue.

As we walked back across campus, hand and hand, a single dark cloud drifted into the sky of happiness in my heart.

"Oh no…" I gasped at my realization.

"What?" She stopped walking.

She became concerned as tears welled up in my eyes again.

"What is it? What's wrong?"

"I… I failed my genetics final exam. I'm going to have to take the class over again. More stupid fruit flies." A tear trickled down my face at the prospect.

She threw her head back and laughed.

"It's okay—I'll be there to help you."

I pictured us kissing up in the lab…

"I guess I'll get through it then," I smiled at her.

Laurie was right.

"*Tara, trust me, you'll know. This type of thing is built into us… It comes naturally when the time is right.*"

In life, I crave absolute truths. My love for Laurie is an absolute truth, as steady as a star shining night after night.

My first week home, I received a small envelope in the mail with a single piece of paper. It was unmarked where it came from, but I beamed when I opened it and read the three words:

Consider yourself snatched.

LEARNING TO LOVE SPIDERS

by

Sasha Faulks

Sasha Faulks lives in rural Wiltshire where she divides her time between her writing; a part-time job painting furniture; and enjoying life with her three children and chocolate Labrador.

Two of Sasha's novels have been published by Freya Publications, 'Loving Amelie' and 'The Garrrow Boy'. Both are available from Amazon.

Charlotte A Cavatica

It was such a beautiful, important name.

It could have been the name of the first woman allowed to be the president of America or the "real" name of a cool singer like Lady Gaga.

It could have been *your* name, Charlotte, because *you* are beautiful and important. To me.

I didn't think it should have been the name of a spider. Unbeautiful little creatures that they are... well, they *are* little compared to a dog or a bus, but they are big and terrifying in the imagination of a six year old girl with a ten year old brother who liked to startle and upset her by putting spiders in her bed and down the back of her top.

Charlotte (story Charlotte) was once a spider in my schoolbook, and we were supposed to like her, although I could only ever like the pig.

The pig was easy to love: he was cute and cuddly with a person-like face, and no one wanted *him* to die. Spiders die all the time. If you cover them with cups or washed-out yoghurt pots they die in a couple of days. Sometimes they look like they are still alive and ready to pounce on you; other times they are all curled up, their spirits gone off to spider heaven.

My brother died covered up. I took the bed-sheet off him because I thought he might have been like a spider that seems dead but isn't, but my mum kept telling me not to do that. First nicely and then all angry, with tears messing up her face—the tears she cried whenever she glass-tested my skin to see if I had the same sort of spots that were on Davey when he died.

I didn't see any spiders for a while after that, maybe because Davey had brought them all to me and, with him gone, they weren't that bothered with a silly little girl like his scaredy-cat left-behind baby sister anymore. I mean, they wouldn't *choose* to go down the back of my dress without him, would they?

I wanted a day back, just one day, when Davey's fingers, his hand, his arm, were on the other end of the tickling terror down the back of my sweater, when my eyes were tight shut against *"the Invasion of the Spider from Space"* with its snapping jaws and hairy legs. There would be screaming and a telling off for both of us, but by teatime he would still be there in his seat, and Mum's scowl would actually mean she was happier than she is today, when her best smile is just a straight line.

Then a spider came back one evening when I was in bed. It was being lowered from the ceiling on an invisible thread and it stopped, inches from my nose, where it had a good look at me before deciding whether or not it was going to kill me. It made busy movements with its front legs like a butcher sharpening his knives.

Suddenly, it didn't matter to me, and I wasn't afraid. I was outside of myself looking down onto a small thing versus a big one. One of us was David and the other was Goliath. I thought that if Davey wouldn't be afraid, why should I be? The worst thing that could happen was that it would kill me—which would be quick, at least, because of all the spider poison—and then I would see him again, in *real* heaven.

Davey in heaven is one of my best thoughts, after my thoughts of you, Charlotte.

It is a place he would have been surprised to find himself in first because our Sunday school teacher, Miss Grinyer, always said *"you two will never get to heaven"* when we took extra squash. Our places in heaven were always hit and miss because of taking extra squash and other things that offended the Lord, but my mum sends her prayers there, so it must be where he ended up.

I like to think of him as he always was, alive with mischief in a heavenly garden where there are no borders to trample and where the girl angels won't think unforgiveable things about him for putting spiders down their necks.

I still keep spiders under yoghurt pots, but they are my pets. My friends.

Here are some things I've learned about spiders:

One. Spiders are not partial to solid food. In fact, a spider only eats liquid food, which suits her very well indeed and she thrives and survives on this and doesn't get any grief from other members of the creepy crawly kingdom for the life choice she has made. She may look spindly in a certain light and in need of a good square meal, but give her a job to do like making a brilliant new web (which she does every day) and she will find the energy. I suppose she decides what's worth fighting for, and when she's done she can choose to hang like a spent thing with no interest in what's going on in the rest of the world around her until she's ready to spin (or suck her lunch) again.

That's the thing about a spider, she is her own woman. Like you, my strong and spindly Charlotte.

Two. Spiders are programmed not to worry too much about their brothers. Or their sisters, for that matter. They are born with lots, so that if one brother gets squashed, or covered in deadly spots, and dies, there is another one (or two, or three, or four or... ooh, *stacks*) to take his place. The life of a spider sister is very straightforward, and never lonely; and the life of a spider mum is not described as *"not worth living, not anymore, without him, not really"* if she loses one of her spider children, because she is busy spinning her heart out to catch flies for the living ones.

Three. A spider knows how to deal with an annoying man.

Davey used to say rhymes like *"boys are it and girls are shit"* but he would stand between me and the worst of the name-callers and the chewing-gum-in-my-hair-stickers at school. I don't think he would have grown up to be as bad as the boys who were scattered around *you*, Charlotte, like the crusts off your sandwiches—crusts that even *I* wouldn't eat for you, if you begged me, because they were dry and dull, and would have tasted of nothing but disappointment. A spider has to have a mate from time to time. It seems it's just the way things are; otherwise there would be no brave Daveys, no beautiful Charlottes and no dumb Daisys in the world. But the cleverest thing a spider does, I think, is to do sex with a mate and then put him in the blender for tea.

I have a spider in the room with me today. She is tiger-striped and quite amazing: she travels about the kitchen on a zip wire. I think she is interested in my cake which is cut into two pieces. One for me and one for you.

I won't let you down, though, Charlotte. I will eat both pieces.

Come to think of it, the boys called you "spider girl" when you came back from your holiday abroad with your legs turned brown and your hair in all those dreadlocks; and I thought *ha*! because that was what I might have called you if I had had a longer time to think about it. But not in a nasty voice, like they did.

They preferred you when you had bigger boobs, because boys are like that, but I love you better the way you are now. You like your bones better than your boobs, so *I* do too. Besides, if you were a spider, I reckon big boobs would get in the way of your zipping and web building.

The boys made love bruises on your neck when they still fancied you. I noticed them when we were in the girls' loos and I held your bag for you because you didn't want it putting down on the dirty wet floor.

"Shit, Daisy, how will he ever fancy me if I look like the side of a house?" you said.

"Why should he fancy you anyway?" I thought. I still think that. He was our teacher: it wasn't his job to fancy you. The boys fancying you was bad enough.

Also, the side of my house is fairly massive, but not much bigger than the house from any other angle. And nowhere *near* as lovely as you. Because you *are* lovely, Charlotte. Your skin is the best; your hair goes blonde and dark in all the right places. Every fashionable thing looks good on you. I would hold your bag out of the wee on the loo floor forever and a day if you asked me to.

I told you that being sick is the easiest peasiest thing in the world: you stick your fingers down your throat and *"hello again macaroni cheese with sausage pieces"*. Hey presto, you get to stay at home with your mum's eyes on you all day.

It made you *feel* sick, but not enough to *do* sick. So you took some of those tablets that make you poo. I was sad that my clever sicking-up trick didn't work on you, but I was happy that we spent most of our lunchtime together, and you said a kind thing to me along the lines of "it's not nice that everyone calls you Crazy Daisy" while you watched me eat up all our crisps and Babybels and chocolate bars on the school steps, away from everyone.

I am going to write the next time I can visit you on my calendar.

The first time I came to see you was the best, because you were very funny about how you were going to hide your food, and we were like the wizard girls who share dorms in Harry Potter, planning adventures. You let me use the hair straighteners on you, and *he* wasn't around, creeping about like creeping Jesus (as my Nan would say) and neither were any other girls from school because they had all stopped liking you by then, same as the boys. It was how I always dreamed it would be: just me and you behind a door we could lock if we wanted to.

The second time was the worst because you had a tube in your nose and you didn't laugh when I opened my bag and poured your soup into it.

The other times get mixed up in my head. I hate it when I turn up and he's there and you let him stay but I can't. I don't understand that about you, Charlotte. He is not a proper friend to you: he never brings a bag for the food with him, for a start.

Today's spider is interested in our cake. Maybe the chocolate pieces remind her of flies.

I wrote on my calendar the next time I could visit you but my mum rubbed it off. Luckily we do appointments in pencil, but I get really cross when things change about. It was on there for days, and then she had a phone call and rubbed it off, just like that.

"Charlotte isn't well enough for visits, anymore," she said, but I think that's a lie—I can hear a lie in people's voices, like "Charlotte's only using you, you stupid bitch" or "I have to see Charlotte to talk about her maths." You didn't like maths; you only liked wasting our precious time with the maths teacher.

No matter how much you hate spiders and brothers, you don't *actually* want them to die, even if you sometimes think it really hard.

Maybe *he* will die now, creeping Jesus, like Davey did, under a sheet. Or a really big yoghurt pot.

Now my spider is hanging like a person on a trapeze at the circus waiting for us to clap. This can also mean she's dead, Charlotte.

We'll have to wait and see.

Charlotte A Cavatica is the name of the fictional spider in E. B. White's 1952 story "Charlotte's Web".

ROLLER COASTER OF WAITING

by

Olga Guymon

Olga Guymon - originally from Moscow, Russia, now lives in New Mexico, U.S.A. with her spouse Teri and their children. Her favorite things in life are her family, nature, visual arts and literature. In addition to her career in criminal justice, she writes poetry and short stories. She dedicates this story to her beloved Teri & Kyle.

In my dream, I was resting in the familiar green field, watching the white puffy clouds passing by. I was probably eight or nine... my mom was expecting my baby brother and I was wondering what he was going to look like... My mom had passed away almost ten years earlier and I missed her...

Something brushed against my cheek, and for a split second I thought it was the tall grass I was hiding in and touched it to move it away, just to find the familiar hand gently rested on my shoulder, lovely fingers against my skin. I smiled and placed my hand over yours, half-opening my eyes. I was back in our home, in bed still—I was just dreaming a moment ago. When did I fall asleep?

"What time is it, love?" I asked. I could not believe it was already past three.

"You felt tired," you responded.

We came back at about noon, so I must have fallen asleep after taking a nap with you. It was the procedure day, and it seemed that many things in the past ten months we've called a "procedure". I've been a centre of attention, sort of, as we've been moving forward to completing our family unit. No simple cosy words came to my mind about what happened today. None of these cold clinical terms—insemination, conception, implantation—gave me a soft feeling about you. None of them could describe the way I felt about you and about our desire to raise a child together. I was almost certain that you felt the same way. We just needed to get off this roller coaster. As I moved a little closer and placed my arm around you, feeling your chest rise quietly under my cheek, I remembered what happened that day.

We got up early and drove to the clinic. We waited for an hour for our "sample" to be prepared. We then had the procedure done in the office, as harsh white fluorescent lights shone above. I stared at the boxes of surgical gloves stacked up in the glass cabinet, counting the boxes of small sizes, then of medium and large ones. My eyes then drifted over to the tiles on the ceiling, as the doctor and two nurses were getting busy to assist us with creating a new life. You did not hold my hand as you did the very first time, months ago. But I felt your presence anyway, despite the distraction of counting objects in the room.

It was a silent procedure this time. The doctor did not say much except, "Let's hope that it works," at the end, and we drove home after a few minutes of rest, just like the last time. You were convinced that getting home and making love was a must for a successful outcome, as we did the last time, when it did work. You made it special while I took a quick shower. You closed the curtains and lit a candle, and got into our bed naked, waiting for me. We later fell asleep, still embracing each other, just like the last time. Tears began to roll down my cheeks and you held me tighter, assuring me that everything would be fine. Everything had to be fine this time.

It's been four months since we lost our baby, our baby-bean, as some would call it: not quite a foetus yet, by medical standards, but our eight-week old baby to us. It was the second procedure that worked, worked like magic, we later thought, still in disbelief and happy in shock. We went on vacation shortly after the procedure. Time flew by as we spent the entire week in the amusement parks, riding on some insane rides and laughing non-stop, concerned just a bit—what if? What if the rides would hurt something? We were not exactly sure about it, and decided to enjoy it and not to worry. I took a home pregnancy test too soon, about ten days after the procedure, just before going on the rides. Negative, so off we went, up toward the sky, down into the tunnels and caves, surrounded by drunken pirates, screaming monsters and all kinds of creatures with names unknown. We returned to the hotel, still laughing, wanting to hold hands but instead pretending to be just friends walking through the palm trees alley, as you were, as usual, too shy to exhibit much affection in public. Down the alley we went, occasionally bumping into each other gently, my hand brushing against your back for a second, here and there, our fingers touching accidentally... I pretended that there was a reason for all that shyness, that we had just met an hour ago, when we shared that last roller coaster ride. On the ride we moved closer to each other as we went down into the darkness at some ridiculous speeds, into the starry sky, not even imagining the possibility of a stop.

We could not stop at that point, I was thinking... We reached to each other for comfort, as two scared children, holding hands in the darkness, putting on our fearless masks afterwards, laughing that it was just fun, of course. We decided to go and spend the rest of the evening together, both outsiders of this town... so I pretended.

You had to stop me at the crosswalk, as I was continuing to daydream about you being my perfect stranger of the night. We crossed to our hotel and were finally alone inside, safe. On our last night of vacation you wanted to visit the swimming pool. I watched you swim silently, occasionally splashing in the dark water. I watched as you swam across the reflections of hotel lights and the moon. I watched you get out, shivering slightly as your skin felt the cool air. I watched your tall body, glistening from water, white under the night lights, your long legs moving fast, running toward the hot tub. I watched you close your eyes once in the warm water, relaxed and comfortable at last. I opted to stay out of the water and kept you company from a white plastic chair. Some gut feeling inside was telling me to stay out of this chlorinated water, even though the tub seemed inviting and you tried to convince me to join you.

The next morning we left early and started the twelve-hour drive home. We stopped at an Indian shop and I bought another rock amulet for good luck. Once we made it back, we both crashed to sleep, exhausted. The next day was Monday. Barely awake, I told you that I was going to pee on a stick again—such a funny way of describing pregnancy testing, but we were used to this terminology by then. I briefly and impatiently glanced at the test stick, negative again, and went back to bed. I heard you exclaim something in excitement a few minutes later. You climbed back into bed with that thing in your hand.

"I see two lines," you said.

I wasn't sure I'd heard you correctly.

"What?"

"I see two lines," you repeated. Later you made fun of my reaction, saying my face exhibited utter shock. We sat in bed staring at the second very faint line for a while.

I didn't know if it was a psychological reaction to knowing that I was pregnant, but the morning sickness came in full blast pretty soon. I followed directions by calling the doctor's office and telling them that the insemination worked. I was told to come in for an ultrasound in two weeks: another standard procedure. I went without you, as you had to work. The doctor was wearing his suit and a tie, which was odd, considering that I was a patient, wearing just some flimsy flowery gown. I felt like it was strange to be there being probed again, and there was no other reason for it, other than following their procedure and paying my co-pay. I felt like I just wanted to be home, nurturing our tiny speck of life inside me, instead of doing this follow-up. But I selfishly wanted to see our baby.

"There is a baby in there," stated the doctor, handing me a picture, pointing at the large black area of the print with some white in it. The smaller area nearby was apparently another baby that "didn't take"—so I learned about a vanishing twin, and it made me sad. It made us both sad, to know that there was possibly an attempt at two lives and that something went wrong with one of them. The oddest thing we learned was how common and probably unknown to so many people that was. We were told that most people do not routinely do ultrasounds so early, most people being husband-wife couples without issues. Our "issue" was that we were two women wanting to raise a child together. Our other issue, so we were told, was my "advanced maternal age", which I understood was anything beyond thirty-five. Therefore we were treated at the only fertility clinic in town, where two doctors were playing God, in a way, and we knew of no other acceptable-to-us way of adding to our family.

My heart was jumping up and down with excitement when I sent the photo of our baby embryo to your phone, and I could hardly wait to get home. You'd already bought the pregnancy journal, and there I pasted our very first picture and wrote that the heartbeat was one hundred and twenty beats per minute. I was to repeat the ultrasound in two weeks: another mandatory procedure, to ensure everything was OK. Two weeks went by, and again I went to get checked. While getting ready, I chatted with a nurse about the morning sickness, and about what I could do about it, as it was getting worse. She suggested a pressure points bracelet and I was interested to try. I wanted to try anything to make it better. The nurse suggested some ginger ale. She was inquiring about our blended family and how our older children took the news about having a sibling. And I told her that we hadn't told our children yet. She wanted to know more about them, so we chatted some while waiting on the doctor. Our children were from our previous marriages, I told the nurse, ages ranging from ten to fifteen. I shared that our children were encouraging us to have a baby together, and I also shared about how my step-kids were like my own and that I had known them now for over five years.

The doctor finally came in. He checked the chart and stated that I was eight weeks. I already read that the baby was about the size of a grape. I didn't mind the ultrasound. The doctor said that at about ten weeks or so, they would "graduate" me to regular prenatal care. I was fine with that. I was fine with whatever needed to be done. I was fine to be there and excited to get another picture to show you.

It didn't hit me right away that something was wrong. The doctor stated that he couldn't find the heartbeat and that we were going to change the ultrasound machines. I thought that the machine was broken somehow and didn't even question a bad possibility. I walked into another room, equipped with a more advanced technology, and not even for a second imagined what happened next. I was pregnant and felt pregnant, and our baby was going to be called a foetus in two weeks... Then the words came.

"You lost this pregnancy... sometime a week or two ago, probably right after your first ultrasound... the baby didn't grow since." The words cut into the air and stiffly fell into my heart, stabbing painfully. Suddenly everything felt out of place: me in this office chair, still feeling nauseous from morning sickness but no longer pregnant; my dead embryo that went to join his or her vanished sibling was still inside me; and I was overcome with a feeling of emptiness and how surreal everything seemed.

The doctor gave me an option to either miscarry the baby naturally or to have a surgical removal. He pointed out that he'd already warned me about my advanced maternal age and about my "old" eggs. That didn't help... I was trying to get distracted by thinking that our doctor didn't have a background in psychology, and that counselling grieving patients was not his forte. Two weeks ago his clinic staff was congratulating us and in such short time we already got used to the idea of becoming parents again. Two weeks later there I was sitting in the same office, trying to absorb the devastating news of losing this pregnancy...

I was somewhat comforted by thinking of what my mom would say to me... I imagined her hand patting me on the back, just like she did when I was little and felt bad about something. I imagined her just being there, reassuring me with her presence only, and I knew that she would feel my pain about her unborn grandchild and would feel the same, without analysing why this happened or judging in any way.

The doctor handed me another picture and asked me if I wanted to keep it. I stared at the image of my dead baby-bean and could not believe that I was offered such a keepsake. With emptiness in my heart I left the clinic and went home. I was told to come back in a week for a scheduled surgery, if I chose to do that. For a week we read everything possible and contemplated getting a second opinion. Our fertility doctor had a great reputation in town. Still, we were hopeful that maybe he was wrong... Some crazy thoughts were coming into my mind, and I was regretful of ever doing that first ultrasound... what if it hurt the baby... I felt guilty about going on that vacation and about the rides.

A week later we went back and I had the surgery. We also wanted answers about what happened and agreed to genetic testing. You were sweet and supportive when you took me home. Groggy and in pain after the procedure, I felt scared to even think of ever trying again. We had kids after all. We were blessed to have them and having another one now, together, was possibly not realistic and was even crazy, perhaps. I was wondering how many couples out there were trying for another child together, after years of learning how to be a divorced parent, or finally finding that special person in their life and realizing that adding to the family might now take some time, if it ever happens. How many people out there, like me, were questioning how in the world you get to the point of your life when you are most happy, and most ready to raise a child, and that is when it is less likely to happen, for whatever reason. Ironically, how much less complicated it was to bring a child into the world in a relationship that didn't last... We were so lucky to have each other and the children that we already had, still wishing to complete our family with one more...

With those kinds of thoughts, I was not really resolving anything, more so going in circles. Again and again I was trying to justify why we were fine in our family unit just the way it was, that having our children we already had was just great, and so on... You brought me the heating pad to relieve pain, and soon the prescribed medication began to work. All I wanted was to sleep and not think of the sadness associated with losing this pregnancy.

Four months after our loss we tried again. Since the genetic testing came back inconclusive, I was certain that there was nothing wrong with me. I had perfectly fine kids (well, teenagers) after all. But either way, I did not wish to hear again that everything happens for a reason, nor did I wish to be judged simply because we wanted to have a child together. I prepared myself mentally for another discussion with the doctor about my old eggs, and again we went to the same clinic. It was a silent procedure this time and then we went home right away. Everything had to be fine... later, we took a nap and I had a dream of the green field from my childhood...

It didn't work. Every pregnancy test was negative and it was becoming clearer that it would be negative every day. After using up all of the dollar-store pregnancy tests and the few brand-name ones left, I gave up, tired of looking at the one line, which remained the same single line for days. I called the doctor and told him that I needed a break. He replied that without medication I had only a slim five to seven per cent chance to conceive anyway, and that we could now move on to some medicated cycles. Our insurance co-pay was not going to cover more of those procedures, so we chose not to go back to the fertility clinic. We decided to embrace our family the way it was and stay happy for each other.

The day I found our midwife was just a couple of months later. It was by accident that I found her name, just looking up some information online. I came across her name and number, and her list of services included artificial inseminations, in small print among all the other things she did for her patients. It was a strange immediate feeling of significance of that small bit of information, like I already knew then that finding her was a link to something unimaginable. I called you and told you that I found someone... that maybe we could try once again and that, imagine that, we didn't have to go to back to the fertility clinic. There was nothing wrong with me, I believed. Well, "old eggs", he said. But our biggest issue was finding someone who could help with the procedure; our second goal would be to find that perfect donor again.

I called the midwife. She answered. She existed—it wasn't an old number, and she was still in business and didn't move, and she did do "those kinds of procedures" amongst all the other things she did. She agreed to meet us in her home office. A week later we were there, chatting with her about each other, our kids, and our desire to have another. The midwife was understanding and very kind, and positive to the point that I almost believed that we could maybe conceive on our own, without anybody's help. We couldn't, of course, but she was that convincing that things should work out. My old eggs were forgotten somehow. You warned me of having false hopes and I assured you that I knew that it might not work, and that I would stay happy no matter what. That was it, the most important thing I learned during that time, to follow my gut feeling about what felt comfortable and right for me, for us, and always remember that we were a family already and were going to stay a family regardless of the outcome of this journey.

We chose the donor again, anonymous and with perfect background and medical history. I asked to try with medications. At home, I charted and wrote things down, before and after work, in between our regular life happenings. It was an easy procedure, in a small pretty room without fluorescent lights and medical cabinets, and it didn't work. We went again the following month, without any medication this time. Again, I charted and timed. Again our specimen was delivered to the midwife's doorstep. We went twice that day. I still remember watching the midwife retrieve the miniature plastic container, with what looked like just a drop of light pink. She ensured the correct labels and offered that I hold the tiny capsule in my hand, to bring it to body temperature. It was odd at first but for the minute that I held it, I closed my eyes and made a wish. You were holding my hand. After the procedure we stayed for a while. During our past experiences at the clinic we left almost immediately, each time, as the doctor ensured us that there was no reason to stay any longer, other than having some psychological benefit. We stayed at the midwife's for maybe a half hour—she left us alone—and after some time passed, you became uneasy and wanted to go home. Just in case, we did the procedure twice that day.

Then the waiting period began all over. We didn't go on any vacation this time, nor did I worry or take tests every other day. I chose to be happy no matter what, and so the days went by quick, with me barely noticing them, staying busy and expecting nothing more than what I'd already gotten in my life. That morning I took a test while you were in the other room. I was intending to leave the testing stick for you, and just glanced at it on my way out. It had two lines, without a doubt. I couldn't stay composed after that: I yelled, "Guess what, honey, you won't believe it!"

You came running and there we were, sitting together again staring at the two lines, clearly there were two of them. You were slightly annoyed, in a teasing way, that I looked at the test first even though "we made a deal" that you would be the one to check it. My defence was that I barely glanced, and there it was… We called the midwife; she ordered some blood work. Our pregnancy was confirmed and the due date set, again. I was worried and so were you. I bled some and went to do another early ultrasound. Everything was fine. We went through a month, then another, then passed the scary eight-week mark. At nine weeks we told our children about expecting their sibling. They were happy to hear the news. We continued to carry on with our lives and expectations until our son, our precious boy, arrived. His siblings adore him, and he will be a year old in March.

The other day, I had a dream that my mom got to meet him...

MORGAN LE FEY

by

Josie Teresi

Josie Teresi is an American writer, psychotherapist and university educator who truly believes in the power of magic to transform, transfix and sometimes even teleport us. She lives with her own Guinevere in a suburb of Camelot, also known as northeast Ohio. She can be found coaching her son's football team, volunteering for her daughter's Girl Scout troop or climbing roofs to rescue one of her two tuxedo cats. "It's never a dull second when we allow ourselves to be in the magic of each moment."

You know me as Morgan Le Fey, evil seductress and sorceress, who devoted her life to the ultimate demise of King Arthur's court. This vicious portrayal of my character betrays my true persona of a gentle woman whose unfortunate fate led her to a lover's betrayal that ultimately ruined her. It is true that I am a scorned woman, but it is not for the reasons that history reflects. For we know that history is dominated by men, who will slant the truth to maintain their egos. I want you to know my story, a story whose harsh lesson shattered my spirit yet cast me towards immortality.

I was the youngest daughter of Lady Igraine and Gorlois, the Duke of Cornwall. My parent's love was the kind that poets envied, but their devotion took an unfortunate turn when a wretched man by the name of Uther Pendragon fell in love with my mother. To gain her affection, Uther enlisted the help of the warlock Merlin to create a pill to disguise him as my father. Unknowingly, my mother lay with him and they conceived a child. In an attempt to become the sole owner of her heart, Uther arranged for my father's murder, and somehow persuaded my mother to marry him. The child they conceived was Arthur, the future King of England.

After their marriage, my mother sent me to a convent to keep me safe from the lecherous eyes of my stepfather. Happiness finds me these years as I discover an affinity for the art of magic and my practice carries with it a gladness to be in union with nature. Unfortunately, my contentment is surrendered when I am betrothed to a foul man named Urien, a close ally to Uther. Further insult pervades as I am forced to become a Lady-in-Waiting for Queen Guinevere, whose counterpart embodied the very essence of my bitterness and resentfulness. This is where I begin my tale.

The early morning of my first day is dreary like my mood as I am set before the Queen as her personal abigail. My obligations include the most intimate of duties of dressing her and I am greatly confused as to why I am placed at this personal detail being so newly appointed. The sun has not yet risen as I wait for the Queen in her personal chambers. I have been instructed to prepare her bath for she likes to wash after she wakes. I savour the warm water as my hand slowly stirs the bath but an odd feeling falls over me as if I am being watched. I glance up to see a fair-haired woman with her intense green eyes focused on me.

"Good morning." I pull my arm from the bath and awkwardly curtsy to her. She nods and I am surprised by the Queen's striking beauty.

"You are Morgan, betrothed wife of Urien?" she asks.

"Yes." I oblige my eyes to meet hers and avoid noticing the outline of her supple body underneath her sheer night-covering. She slides each strap of her night-dress down her shoulders and allows it to slip to the floor. As she stands fully nude in front of me, I frantically dart my eyes away and scurry to the other side of the room to straighten some linen. She steps into the bath and settles in with no reservations. My eyes are soon drawn back to her as water streams down her full breasts and firm belly. Her mouth opens slightly as she washes her slender neck.

"Morgan," she calls. I set aside the linen and approach the bath. She offers me the washing cloth and her fingers linger on mine as I extend my hand to receive it. She pulls her long hair to the side and turns to present me her smooth back. With long strokes, I tenderly wash her, yet shame fills me as I compel myself to remember that this very woman still represents all that I scorn. I pull my arm back as though burned by a flame and she notices my sudden withdrawal.

"Are you well?" she asks.

"Yes, your Majesty," I reply, as I suck in a deep breath to contain myself. "What should I prepare you to wear?"

"My Mistress of Robes already put aside my attire for this day."

"I am confused—for what, then, are my services to you?" My brow furrows as natural annoyance finally fills me.

"What services would you like to provide for me, Mistress Morgan?" Her lips form a brazen smile as she caresses her neck. The purpose of her coyness is not clear to me and I refuse to be pulled into her provocative game.

"I would like to be released from my duties, for I would rather attend to swine than to be forced to honour your court." Her mouth now hangs open as we are both shocked by my churlish retort. I stand firm yet my knees tremble as I wait for her response.

"Why do you think such ill of me?" Her eyes reflect genuine hurt. "I was not the one to murder your father for my own selfish gain. Arthur and I may be joined in marriage but we are not the same person." She steps out of the bath and wraps a towel around herself. Her body leaves a trail of dripping water as she returns to her bedchamber without looking back. Her disclosure surprises me, as I did not know she was aware of my connection to Arthur. Soft whimpers creep out from her slightly open chamber door and I pad softly over. The Queen sits on a majestic bed with her hands covering her face and I wonder why is she crying? What am I to her?

Pushing the door open, I sit next to her and brush away a damp lock from her face. She sniffles and wipes her eyes to collect herself. Entwining her hands as if in prayer, she settles them on to her lap and I find it difficult not to succumb to her beauty as her jade eyes settle on mine. A sudden flash of yearning in my womanhood embarrasses me.

"I beg your pardon for my rude conduct, your Majesty," I say. "I have allowed the dreaded past to darken my current perception of you and so I ask for another chance to remain your humble attendant." I hold my breath until she answers.

"I would like for you to remain in my services." She takes my hands. "You do not know that I have been your admirer since I first saw you at the convent in Siciles tending to one of the luscious gardens. The beauty of that garden suited you well, for you were so content within its arms." My heart flutters at this declaration and I gaze at her crimson lips as she forms every precious word. She continues, "Intrigued by your innocence, I learned of the reasons for your admittance to the holy community and resolved that the Kingdom owes you penance for the crimes of Arthur's father." At that moment, my bitterness is released and I vow my service to this fair Queen.

The following months confirm my dedication to her. I soon become her primary attendant despite the jealous discernment of the other abigails, whose experience in such dealings far surpasses my own. As her constant companion, we travel together to foreign lands when she finds it necessary to personally deal with political diplomacy. She has earned a shrewd reputation that garners respect from many kingdoms. When in our homeland, the Queen and I only separate when the moon rises and she has to submit to her duties as wife to Arthur. It is during these hours of darkness that the ivy of jealousy envelops me as I think about him touching her how I desire to touch her. I suppose that I should reserve these thoughts for my future husband, but I avoid any physical affections whenever he visits, for I am repulsed by him. It is only Guinevere that I want.

Late one evening, as the frost gathered on the sills of the castle windows, I awake to the creaking of my chamber door opening. I pull the linens tighter to cover myself and instantly sit up. My heart pounds as I soon realise that it is Guinevere softly entering my room.

"My Queen, is everything all right?" I reach for a candle to see her clearer. She stands looking vulnerable and sad and I step from my bed to reach her. "My lady, please tell me what is the matter?" She says nothing, but her eyes say everything and my heart melts. I feel drawn to kiss her but dare not. She finally speaks.

"You must leave the Court," she whispers. Her words pierce the air like an arrow and I am struck hard by them.

"Why, your majesty, have I displeased you in some way?" My eyes fill with tears while my throat feels as though a noose encircles it.

"You don't realise, my sweet Morgan, how this wretched castle can ruin you!" Tears now fill her eyes and I bravely guide her to my bed. We sit and she deliciously curls into my lap. Stroking her pale hair, I savour her closeness, as I long to gather her up inside me to protect her. Despite her demurred persona, I see all her insecurities and want to heal them. I draw her up to my bosom and hold her as her tears fall. She nestles deeper into me and I know she must be able to hear my heart pound. She gently pulls my face to hers and kisses me full on the lips. I return the gesture and kiss her back fervently as all my senses blur into one. I soon feel like flames engulf me as I am overwhelmed by the reality of this moment.

She breaks from my mouth and kisses a sensuous path from my neck to my ear. Her sultry breath teases me as she whispers, "Only you can calm me, Morgan." I gasp softly and feel the tension build more intensely in my womanhood. She trails kisses back to my mouth and we continue to savour the taste of one other. I eagerly succumb to my desire for her as we melt together. She is so exquisite and I crave for her to reach deep inside and hold me there forever in our ecstasy.

The early morning light sneaks into the room as my fair Queen begins to stir from sleep. I kiss her forehead and her radiant eyes stare into my own and I have to remind myself that I am not dreaming.

"I do not wish to ever leave you," I softly whisper. Sadness fills her eyes as she pulls the bed linens snugly around her and glances away from me. A large cold breeze rushes into the space between us as she leaves the bed to slip back into her night-dress.

"We must not tell anybody about our affections for one another," she says coolly. My heart sinks even though she approaches to kiss my cheek. I am saddened by her sudden withdrawal as she departs to return to her chambers before Arthur awakes.

That day begins with our usual routine but she displays no emotion or affection toward me and I do my best not to show my distress. She chooses to dress alone and I return to my chamber to grieve this apparent dismissal.

After a few moments, I collect myself and return to the Queen's chambers. Before I enter the room, I can hear Arthur's distinct voice through the closed door.

"I do not understand your dealings with her." Arthur's voice echoes loudly. "Your duty was to persuade her to harness her powers for the benefit of this Kingdom, not for her to become your personal pet." I press my ear closer to the door for I am not clear on the subject of their conversation.

"I am sorry, Arthur," Guinevere replies. "I will ensure her full cooperation with this matter but please do not refer to her as my pet. Her inherent innocence shields her from such apparent misguidings and I find these qualities endearing."

"You are a fool if you dare fall for such gullible trappings, woman!" Arthur growls. "I have been patient enough and I demand that you compel her to become this kingdom's sorceress. Her reputation proves that her powers are equal to that of Merlin's, and I will become the sole proprietor of her enchantments." Silence now deafens the space between them and I rush away because I cannot bear to hear anymore.

I burst through my chamber door and plummet onto my bed, the same bed where we bared our fervent desires just the night before. I whimper softly into my pillow as I digest the harsh words that fell upon my ears. I cannot bear to think that Guinevere's affections are not genuine. How would she be able to look me in the eye if betrayal was her plan? Were her tears only the shadow of guilt in disguise? The more I wonder, the angrier I become.

My tears soon turn to rage as the veil has been lifted and I see that I have been made a fool. I took my duties as the Queen's lady very seriously and wanted my genuine abilities to represent my loyalty to the Kingdom, so I refused to do magic of any kind. Moreover, to discover that the very thing I kept hidden was the prize they were coveting. I could destroy this Kingdom with a wave of my hand if I so chose. Like lightning slicing through the dark of night, the image of Guinevere's face, ravished with ecstasy from our previous night's lovemaking, flashes in my mind. I snap my hands to cover my eyes as a feeble attempt to block this taunting image. I love her yet hate her equally.

A light knock on my door startles me. I take a moment to collect myself before answering.

"Morgan? Morgan? It is your Queen. May I enter?" Just the sound of her voice feels like a slap to my face yet my heart still yearns for her.

"Yes, my Queen." I briefly hesitate to open the wooden barrier separating myself from her.

"Are you okay?" Her eyes meet mine and I refuse to let her know my anguish.

"Yes." I hold my breath and stand firm as she studies me.

"I am truly sorry for my rude behaviour earlier," she says. I search her eyes for any clue to her pending betrayal. She quickly turns away and awkwardly looks about my chamber as if she read my thoughts. I say nothing in response. She glances back to me and I feel small under her stare. I inhale and obstinately remain distant, as I will not allow myself to fall victim to her manipulations again. She steps to me and takes my hand to place it on her heart. I cannot resist the heat of her touch and desperately try to fight the urge to fold into her. She is like a scorpion that stings me yet it is only her venom that can save me. "Morgan, I do adore you," she says. "You command my thoughts more than you are aware. There is something about your innocence that I want to breathe in and savour, for I have never met another who affects me like you do." She lifts my chin and sweetly kisses me. Although I am the enchantress, she is the one who places a spell on me, and I am helpless to dispel it. Once again, I want her.

My passion for her is vicious as I spin her and press her to my bed. Straddling her, I capture her arms above her head so she cannot touch me. She writhes beneath me as I bite into the tender flesh of her neck, marking my territory. She lets out a cry and I can see lust reflected in her eyes. My purpose is to punish her for making me a fool in her game that I simply cannot resist to play. I rip at her garments and fiercely enter her. She embraces me tighter and tighter as my hand thrusts into her womanhood, which is like dripping velvet. When she is about to reach the crest of her yearning, I completely pull myself from her and force her to meet an unrelenting frustration. This utter lack of engagement infuriates her, yet drives her to me, as she snatches the back of my head and propels my mouth toward hers. I feel as if I can barely breathe, as she allows no time to gather air between our kisses. A harsh knock on the door snaps us out of our fervent dance and we break away, only to be left panting like animals.

"Your Majesty?" The voice remains from behind the door and belongs to Deborah, one of the Queen's elder servants.

"Yes, Deborah," Guinevere replies between breaths as she gathers her tattered garments.

"The King is requesting your presence in the main hall to meet the Duke of Siciles." I quickly smooth out my dress and press down my dishevelled hair as Guinevere reviews the damage done to her attire.

"Let the King know that I will be there momentarily. Oh, and Deborah, can you please bring my receiving dress?" There is a brief pause before Deborah responds.

"Um, your Majesty, would you like for me to bring it to you here at this chamber?" I hold back a snicker, as I am eager to see how Guinevere will respond to Deborah's apparent curiosity.

"Yes, Deborah, bring it here to me, for Mistress Morgan will assist me in my preparation for the Duke." A triumphant smirk slides across her lips as I toss her a contentious look. I am still so angry with her, angry that she can mesmerise me with her eyes, her smile, her touch, her scent, and, shall I dare say, her glorious body.

The weeks that follow lead me back into my regular duties to the Queen even though I battle with the notion of abandoning the Court all together just for the sake of self-preservation. The Queen and I show no outward traces of affection, though I often feel the heaviness of her stare on me and I cannot help but wonder what thoughts possess her. She still has not mentioned what this Kingdom's true plans are for me. Although her betrayal continues to haunt me, I settled myself on the belief that she is a mere pawn in Arthur's plan to harness my magical power. It is true that I am as powerful as Merlin, for I was his apprentice during my time at the convent. I also know that Merlin and Arthur have distanced themselves from one another for reasons that are unclear to me. In all candour, there is a piece of me that wants to be this Kingdom's enchantress, but it is not for the reason of serving my half-brother or my country. I am driven by the delusion that I can be the sole possessor of Guinevere's heart and it is this mirage that leads me to my tortured fate.

One day, while the sun fed its warmth to the dripping snow on the barren tree branches, Arthur visited while I was alone folding the Queen's laundered garments. I felt my whole body tense as he approached for I knew that his motives were selfish.

"Morgan Le Fay," he begins with a crooked smile on his vile mouth. "I understand that you possess powers that some say are beyond those of the great wizard Merlin's." His dark eyes stare at me intently as I continue folding without looking up at him. "Is this true?" he firmly barks, apparently annoyed by my ability to ignore his presence. I suck in a deep breath and heave an incensed glare at him.

"It *is* true," I eventually reply, stifling my anger. Folding his arms while pacing, he waits for me to expand on my response, but I do not. I continue to obsessively fold and his agitation grows.

"Your service to the Queen has been adequate, but I feel the utilization of your powers would most benefit this Kingdom." He pauses a moment to study my reaction but I continue my chore without looking at him. "So your duties to my Queen are relinquished, and your sole obligation will be as sorceress to this empire." Trembling, I take another deep breath and slowly exhale as I now struggle to contain my rage.

"What if I refuse?" I stubbornly retort.

"Then you will lose your pretty head," Arthur snaps back as he glides his repugnant fingers down my cheek.

"You are no different than your father," I slap his hand away and snarl. I throw the folded garment at him and stomp away from his hideous presence. I run to search for Guinevere in her personal chamber. Rushing through her door to seek comfort in her arms, I find her in an intimate embrace with one of Arthur's knights, Lancelot. A suffocating gasp chokes out from my mouth as I feel like the last bit of air is forced from my body. Guinevere pushes away the knight and her eyes fall onto my apparent pain. Feeling trapped by these putrid castle walls, I turn and stumble back to my chamber, as my heart feels like it has been crushed by a large boulder.

Entering my room, I am enraged to find Arthur hunting through my belongings. My sudden appearance shocks him and I snatch a book of potions from his hand. His murky eyes narrow as if he wishes to strike me. Guinevere enters behind me. I cannot bear this any longer.

In a moment of utter defeat, I surrender my vow of magical virtue and assault the King with a massive power blast from my fingertips that propels him backwards into the jagged stonewall, rendering him unconscious. Fearing her own safety and realizing the feral look in my eyes, Guinevere slowly backs away as if I am a wild animal. It stings to see her fear me but my anger is unrelenting. Hearing the clamour of violence, Lancelot dashes in and sees Arthur on the ground. He grasps Guinevere's arm and protectively pulls her behind him while raising his sword to defend. I snap a bolt at him that sends his sword twirling across the room. His face drains of colour as he is frozen with fear. He shoves the Queen from the room and panicked footsteps scurry away.

Beguiled by insanity, I set the entire contents of my chamber on fire. I travel through the door toward the rest of the castle, leaving a wake of blazing destruction behind. I am content to let this wretched castle crumble along with all its hideous inhabitants. This is the only way I can escape its suffocating clutches. A peaceful calm settles over me as I stroll from the castle's grand entrance. Many people die from my fiery vengeance, but my intended targets do not. It is at this point that I commit myself to Arthur's ultimate demise.

Think of me what you will, but please know that my evil reputation is undeserved. The wicked culprit that shattered my spirit and ruined me was the vicious betrayal of my love and innocence. Yet it is this malevolent circumstance which catapults me toward the infamy of my immortality. I am Morgan Le Fay.

THE MISSING PIECE

by

Danni Pearson

Danni Pearson is a PhD student with the Open University exploring same-sex couples in long-term relationships. She writes fiction in her spare time and is currently writing her first novel called 'The Truth Behind the Darkness' (working title). Her short story 'The Missing Piece' is a prequel to her novel.

Chapter 1

She awoke from the terrifying nightmare with a gasp. Her body was soaked, glistening with sweat, yet she was freezing cold. Maybe it was the remnants of the unmoving blackness in her nightmare, the suffocating and unrelenting sadness that weighed heavy on her heart. She knew why she kept having this nightmare, night after night. She felt on a spiritual level dreams represented waking thoughts and emotions, and this nightmare embodied the very being of her psyche. The sheer uncomfortable and out-of-place feeling that was her perfect life. Maddie was 25 years old, had a lovely and kind husband, Jeremy, and a gorgeous daughter called Jamie. So why did she feel so uncomfortable in her own skin? Why did she feel this crushing worry that her life was not what she had planned? The darkness of her nightmare was beginning to feel like her companion, the place where she could go deep within herself to make the feelings go away. It was her safety, her solitude and her private fortress.

"Babe, are you okay?" Jeremy asked, turning towards her and stirring from sleep.

"Yes, I just had a nightmare. Sorry I woke you," she replied.

"It's okay, was it the same one again?"

"Yes it was. I'm okay though. Go back to sleep," she encouraged him.

"Okay, night hun," he said quickly, giving her a peck on the cheek.

"Night."

He turned the bedside lamp off and rolled over away from her. Maddie lay frozen on the bed. Her unhappiness was seeping into her behaviour. The moment he touched her, she felt her insides shudder; she tried desperately not to visibly stiffen at his touch but she knew that it was becoming more difficult to hide. She was glad it was dark so he couldn't see her now.

She tried to recall a time when she was happy with Jeremy, truly happy, but this was an increasingly common thought she struggled with. Images flashed across her mind. She was at the beach and heard Jamie's laughter as Jeremy chased her through the sand. Her wedding day seven years ago, when she had said "I do" to Jeremy, surrounded by happy family and friends. The day Jamie was born, with Jeremy by her side, supporting her whilst she went through excruciating labour. She realised these fleeting moments were when she felt truly happy, but they were few and far between nowadays and almost always related to Jamie. She loved Jeremy to bits, but it didn't feel right anymore. He had become more like a best friend and cherished companion rather than her lover and husband. He was safe—he was the only person she had ever been with—and she was deeply unhappy.

She knew she was being unreasonable, that her life was a lot better than most. She wondered how many people could say they had a dream job, a lovely husband and a beautiful daughter. Not many, she thought. It didn't matter though. All the comparisons in the world couldn't help her shake this feeling. She didn't know what this was, it could have been depression. She had suffered from post-natal depression for nearly half a year when Jamie was born. In that period, she had completely disengaged from Jeremy and the outside world. She was glad Jamie had only been two months old and didn't know how bad it had become. There were times when she didn't want to hold her, didn't want to show her happiness or affection, but thankfully it had not affected Jamie's penchant to show affection and love. Maddie had tried her best to fight it when it came to Jamie, but she realised that she didn't try to fight the depression and darkness where Jeremy was concerned, and he just hadn't known what to do. He had been useless and completely helpless.

She glanced at her alarm clock: it read 3:40 a.m. She sighed—this had to stop. She needed to extinguish this nightmare, to conquer the darkness and face her demons. She'd do this tomorrow. For now, though, she would resign herself to the darkness, let it consume her, and bury herself deep within its grasp.

Chapter 2

Maddie awoke with a feeling of regret and shame for the terrible thoughts she'd had last night following her dream. She felt as though she had betrayed Jeremy with her thoughts, felt dirty and unworthy. This was part of the circle in which she found herself. The nightmare would awaken her feelings of darkness, loneliness and unhappiness deep within her heart and soul. The next morning, the light of the day would shake her mind into the rational thought of a moral wife bound by a contract and duty to her husband. Seven years ago, she had agreed to marry her childhood sweetheart because she loved him and wanted to spend the rest of her life with him. Her thoughts the previous night were wrong and a betrayal of her vows. She knew that marriage was not full of constant happiness, that relationships had their ups and downs. This was just a difficult time in their marriage. They would get through this. It was a battle between her head and her heart and it was emotionally draining. She needed to fight the uprising in her heart and the voice in the back of her mind. Her head was stronger, so she told herself it was going to be okay, vowed to fight for the sake of her marriage and her daughter.

*

Maddie entered her office to be greeted by her boss James Garner. He was an older man, just past 60. He was small-framed, pale-skinned, had grey wiry hair and soft grey eyes. He was about a foot shorter than Maddie, but the height difference did not stop him from busting her ass all the time.

"Maddie, where the hell have you been? You're ten minutes late," he berated her.

"Sorry, James, I got caught in traffic taking Jamie to school," she replied.

"Save your mummy stories for some who gives a shit. Now, you have an interview this morning for the Metro. You need to be at

Starbucks in the centre for 10 a.m. Then get your butt back here for a new case. It's fraud, so bring your thinking cap."

"Okay, thanks."

Maddie sighed and went to sit at her desk. She worked as a private investigator at Garners Consulting and Investigations. She'd been here for just over three years now, and loved every minute of it. Her boss was old school. He barked orders, was hard on her, but did it for her development. Two years ago, James had said she was a brilliant PI but needed some experience. He had followed this by more field work, more responsibility and some out-of-town jobs. His motto was clearly "sink or swim" and she had been swimming from the get-go. She admired him for his attitude though: even though he was sometimes grumpy and a hard-ass, he ran a good business and he was a great teacher.

She took a seat at her desk and sighed. If only her passion and love for her job seeped into her love for Jeremy. Her job was the only distraction from the dreams and the darkness. Jamie was the sunlight in her life at home, but her work was the moon, driving her to succeed when she felt other parts of her life were failing. That *she* was failing. She snapped out of it. She needed to prepare for this meeting. This morning she had just thrown on her black trouser suit and pink blouse. She went into the ladies' bathroom to check her appearance.

She examined herself in the mirror. Her brown eyes did not hide her sadness. Her suit looked smart, though. Her black shoes with the slight heel gave her a smart power-woman look. She had long straight brown hair and ivory-coloured skin. She applied some black mascara and eyeliner to her eyes and topped it off with a pale pink blusher to her cheeks. She felt satisfied her face looked alive enough to make a good impression for the meeting and her suit gave a professional look. She exited the bathroom, bid her colleagues farewell and left the office.

Chapter 3

Maddie hurried through the door of Starbucks and then sudden panic hit her. Who the hell was she meeting and what exactly was it for? She had been too apologetic to James to even ask this morning and too distracted by her thoughts to worry. Oh well, she thought, I'm sure if I look lost enough someone will claim me.

"Maddie?" a lady with a soft, husky tone asked.

Maddie turned around to see a tall blonde woman with a friendly smile. She had green eyes and a curvy figure. Wow, Maddie thought, she was beautiful. The mystery woman was dressed in a stylish yet understated pair of denim jeans and a purple tight fitted shirt that complemented her figure. She was stunned to silence. It had been at least 20 seconds since the woman had called her name and she was just staring at her like some weirdo. *Maddie?!* A voice inside her head jolted her back to reality.

"Oh, sorry, I was miles away. Yes, I'm Maddie," she responded.

"Hi, my name is Summer, I'm from the Metro. We have a meeting here at 10.30?"

"Yes, sorry. I just had the sudden realisation that I didn't have a clue who I was meeting so thanks for coming up and getting my attention."

"No problem, nice to meet you," Summer replied politely, and offered her hand out to Maddie.

Maddie grasped Summer's hand in response. A sudden jolt of electricity shot up Maddie's hand and coursed through her veins. She gasped and took her hand away quickly.

"Wow, um, sorry, I think we got an electric shock off each other then," Maddie said quickly.

"Yes, I felt it too," Summer replied with a wry smile.

Maddie looked into Summer's eyes and saw a glint of humour in them, and something else she couldn't put her finger on. Why was she acting so strange around this woman? She had turned into an apologetic and starey loony. She felt her cheeks flush slightly and was glad she'd applied the blusher, hoping her embarrassment didn't show.

"Shall we go find a seat?" Maddie asked nervously.

"Oh yes, of course. I have a sofa for us already. Follow me," Summer replied.

They walked to the back corner of the coffee shop. Summer gestured for Maddie to sit on the brown leather sofa opposite where a black parka was covering part of another sofa. There was an empty mug and several morning newspapers on the table. Summer had obviously been here for a while.

"Please sit there, Maddie. I thought a sofa would be comfy and informal rather than the table over there. Now, what would you like to drink?" Summer asked.

"Can I have a skinny vanilla latte, please? No sugar."

"Sure," Summer replied chirpily. "Be right back."

Maddie turned to the table. She placed her bag on the sofa next to her, and took out her pad and a pen and business card. She took off her suit jacket and placed it folded neatly on top of her bag. Her thoughts idled towards the strange introduction she had just experienced. The electric shock felt like much more than a normal electric shock from static electricity. It had raised her heart rate: she had felt her pulse quicken and her breathing get faster. Something had stirred inside her, made her feel nervous—it was excitement, she thought. Summer had made her feel excited.

"Here you go, one skinny vanilla latte." Summer had returned, and placed the drink in front of Maddie.

"Great, thank you," Maddie smiled.

Summer returned her smile and Maddie's heart rate quickened again. Her stomach fluttered and the nerves were back. Just from one look from this woman. Was it because Maddie was intimidated? This woman was beautiful—perhaps it was envy, or a feeling of inadequacy. She didn't know. Now was not the time to figure it out.

"So, Maddie, do you mind if I ask you a few questions?" Summer said as she seated herself opposite Maddie.

"Shoot," Maddie replied in a friendly tone.

"Okay, so I'll quickly introduce myself properly. I'm a journalist from the Metro and I'm doing a story on PIs. Your boss said you were the best he had," Summer said.

"Wow, well he's never told me that. That's him all over, compliments behind my back!" Maddie laughed.

"Haha, well, he had nothing but nice things to say about you. So far, I would have to agree, you seem very nice and friendly." Summer complimented her. Maddie felt herself blush again.

"Thanks. I thought I was more blithering idiot." she said with nervous laughter.

"Not at all," Summer smiled.

"Good." Maddie returned the smile. "And thank you for being so lovely."

"Look at you, returning my compliment. Thank you," Summer observed playfully. They both laughed.

"So, why don't you start by telling me how you got into private investigative work? Then we'll move onto a few special cases, perhaps?" Summer offered.

"Great. Well I started PI work about three and a half years ago…" Maddie began.

She realised her nerves had now been replaced by a feeling of established comfort. Summer was a charismatic woman, and had managed to settle any nerves by giving Maddie that compliment. Maddie continued with her story in a state of happiness and excitement that this person was interested in her work.

Before she knew it, they were three coffees into her life story, and Maddie had discovered that Summer had moved to Bristol only a few months ago when she had started working at the Metro. Before that, she had worked at a local newspaper in Birmingham. Maddie had concluded that Summer was a graceful lady and someone that she could envisage being good friends with. She thought about how comfortable she felt being around her and how interested she was in every word that Summer said. She hadn't felt that in a long time.

"God, look at the time? It's nearly 12:30—we've been here for two hours. Where did the time go?" Maddie said in a light tone.

"I've no idea, it must have been because we were having so much fun talking," Summer smiled teasingly.

Maddie couldn't tell, but it sounded like there was more to the statement Summer had uttered. She looked at Summer. Summer looked pointedly back at Maddie, and that's when Maddie felt it again. Her pulse quickened, her heart raced and she could hear her raspy breathing. Neither of them said anything, they just sat staring at each other in comfortable silence. There was a tension that Maddie didn't recognise. It was like an electric undercurrent that occurred when they looked at each other.

"That's too true." Maddie broke the silence but not her gaze.

"Shall we wrap it up then?" Summer enquired.

"Yes, I better get back to the office. I have a new case coming this afternoon," Maddie replied

"Okay, well, Maddie, it has been a pleasure meeting and chatting to you. Can I give you my card in case you want to meet again?" Summer smiled. "Although, not to interview you this time," she added.

"Of course, Summer, that would be great. Perhaps we could go out for another coffee some time," Maddie replied. Maddie stood and gathered her things. She gave Summer her card.

"Feel free to call me if you need anything. I know moving to a new city can be pretty scary," Maddie said.

"Yes, it can. It would be nice to have a friend," Summer replied. "I'll look forward to next time."

"Me too." Maddie said.

Summer held out her hand for Maddie to shake. Maddie felt nervous whilst reaching towards Summer's small and soft hand. She grasped it and felt the same feeling as last time. Electricity coursed through her veins and her hand tingled where she made contact with Summer's. This time she was expecting it, so she rode it like a wave rather than denying it. She looked at Summer:

she could tell that this beautiful woman could feel the same sensation. She saw it in her eyes. Realising they had held on a moment too long, Maddie let go. She felt slightly embarrassed by the sensation, nervous about what it meant and stupid for not knowing.

"Goodbye, Maddie," Summer said, with a flirtatious smile on her lips.

"Bye, Summer." Maddie returned the smile and left.

Chapter 4

Maddie lay in bed, wide awake. She and Jeremy had gone to bed hours ago, but she had not slept a wink. Her mind was racing, filled with thoughts of her encounter with Summer. She just couldn't get Summer out of her head—her long, shiny blonde hair, her soulful green eyes, her husky voice and soft laugh. The way she'd felt when they touched hands, how comfortable it had been. The underlying tension she'd felt every time they spoke and looked at each other. She remembered the excitement, her heart racing and breathing quickening. What did it mean? Why couldn't she get her out of her head? What had this woman done to her? There was a connection between them that she had never felt before and a sense of closeness that she didn't believe could exist when she barely knew the person. The thing that had really been keeping her up was the wonder. Maddie did not know what to do now—she wondered if she should call Summer, but didn't know whether it was right. But she also felt like she had to call Summer. She wanted to feel that again, feel the excitement and rush of electricity. She felt that she needed to resolve the feeling so she could get on with her life.

A voice deep within Maddie spoke to her when she thought that. It told her that she couldn't just ignore Summer. The feeling would not be easily resolved. Maddie thought it was the voice of the darkness, the suffocating darkness that invaded her dreams and filled her with sadness. She fought her thoughts, her racing mind and the menacing darkness. She needed to sleep because she was exhausted.

That night she didn't have the nightmare.

*

Maddie was home alone after taking the morning off. She stood in her kitchen, fiddling with the small white business card Summer had given her. The decision had been going around her head for an hour. Should I call her? She decided to bite the bullet and call. It couldn't hurt anyone, could it? *Except Jeremy*, the voice in the back of her mind commented.

"Hello. Summer Harrison," the voice greeted.

"Hi Summer, it's Maddie. Um, Maddie Watkins, from yesterday."

"I know you're from yesterday. I can't forget someone like you easily," Summer flirted.

"Haha," Maddie laughed nervously. "Um, would you like to meet for coffee?"

"Sure, that sounds great. Where?" Summer replied, excitement rising in her voice.

"Well, same place as yesterday, in, say, an hour?"

"Perfect. See you then," Summer responded.

*

Maddie sat in Starbucks nervously playing with her wedding ring. Guilt haunted her, questioning what she was doing. She knew this was wrong, knew this was something more than friendship, but she couldn't stop herself. She looked up to see Summer walking towards her. Today she was wearing a pair of men's jeans and a grey jumper, and she still looked incredible. Summer took a seat opposite her.

"Hey," she greeted.

"Hey, Summer," Maddie replied with a smile. She could already feel the tension between them, the unspoken connection. Her heart was racing and her nerves working in overdrive.

They sat talking for over an hour. Maddie told Summer about her nightmares, the unhappiness she felt being with her husband, but the overwhelming sense of loyalty she had for him and their life together. Summer told Maddie about her past.

"I'm gay, Maddie," Summer said softly.

"I know," Maddie replied. "I could tell from the way you looked at me. Plus, I googled you." She smiled light-heartedly.

"You googled me?" Summer said with surprised laughter.

"Haha, yes I did. I was intrigued." Maddie laughed too.

"It's okay, I googled you before we met. I had to for the interview," Summer winked.

"Oh my, well how rude. At least I met you first and *then* googled you!" Maddie played along.

"So anyway, what did you mean by how I looked at you?" Summer asked.

"Um, well I could see in your eyes. It was attraction. I think. Not that I'm an expert," Maddie replied.

"But you're very observant," Summer noted without denying it.

"I have to be. So what's your story?" Maddie enquired.

"I was engaged to my last girlfriend. We were together for two years. I came home to find her in bed with one of my friends. Safe to say, it was over from then. So I found a job as soon as I could and moved here. It was a year ago. I'm over it now," she stated softly.

"Oh, Summer, I'm sorry, I didn't mean to bring it up," Maddie said hurriedly.

"It's okay."

Maddie reached across the table and touched Summer lightly on the hand in a gesture of comfort. It felt like the right thing to do. Summer responded slightly to Maddie's touch, grasping the end of her fingers with her own. They stayed like it in silence for a couple of minutes. Maddie gazed at Summer meaningfully. Summer turned slightly towards Maddie and began to grip her hand more tightly. Fearfully, Maddie quickly removed her hand away feeling guilt and shame flush her face.

"Sorry, I…" she began.

"No, it's okay," Summer said.

"I'd better be going," Maddie said.

"Yeah, me too. I have work to do," Summer smiled, her eyes concealing the hunger and attraction she felt for Maddie.

Chapter 5

Summer stood in Maddie's kitchen smiling whilst Maddie made them a drink. Maddie had met with Summer for coffee every weekday last week and twice this week. Over the weekend, Maddie was surprised to feel that she missed Summer's company, the open and honest chats they'd had, and the closeness she felt. The tension was growing. Maddie could feel it. Both Jeremy and Jamie had commented on how Maddie seemed happier at home. It just made Maddie feel all the more guilty. Nothing had happened with Summer—they were just friends, they both had stated this. But there was guilt present and Maddie knew that the guilt was due to her hiding the true nature of her relationship with Summer from Jeremy and, more importantly, from herself.

"How has work been?" Summer asked.

"It's been okay, have started working on a surveillance case this week. The fraud case last week came to nothing," Maddie answered.

"Surveillance sounds interesting."

"Yeah, it can be but this one is infidelity paranoia."

"Oh ok. It's not Jeremy, is it?" Summer joked.

"Um, no, Summer. And that's not funny. He hasn't a reason for any paranoia," Maddie retorted sharply.

"Right, sorry. That was rude of me. I'm really sorry," Summer replied hastily.

"It's okay," Maddie assured her.

Maddie looked up and saw that Summer was gazing at her, intent in her eyes. Maddie knew that what she had just said was a lie, that her feelings for Summer were more than just platonic. She could see it in Summer's eyes, too, and the knowing smile that was etched on her face. They shared an unspoken lie, something that Maddie wasn't ready to talk about yet. Summer began to move towards Maddie.

"Maddie," Summer said.

She had crossed the space between them. She brought her hand up and touched Maddie delicately on her arm. She began to move closer still but Maddie took a quick defensive step back.

"What are you doing, Summer? I'm not gay!" Maddie shouted.

"Sorry, I thought," Summer said whilst retreating back further.

"No, you thought wrong."

"Okay. I should go," Summer said.

"Okay," Maddie agreed.

And with that, Summer walked out the door.

*

Maddie knocked lightly on the red door. Summer lived in a modern brick house in an estate on the outskirts of Bristol. It looked beautiful from the outside and Maddie guessed the inside would be just as nice. Although she had known her less than two weeks, she thought this was very Summer. There was a small garden which had flowering yellow and pink roses next to a driveway space for two cars. The door opened slowly to reveal Summer. Her blonde hair was put up in a loose ponytail displaying Summer's light and smooth skin. She smiled when she realised it was Maddie at the door.

"Hey," she said, surprise etched in her voice.

"Hi, Summer," Maddie replied. "I don't really know what I'm doing here."

"It's okay, come on in," Summer said as she gestured for Maddie to follow.

They entered the downstairs hallway, which was decorated a dark red and gold colour. It was very sophisticated, and everything Maddie expected. She followed Summer into a dining room which was warm and welcoming. The whole house was warm and welcoming. There was artwork hung around the walls of flowing meadows and wintry landscapes. *Summer had great taste*, Maddie thought. They entered the spotless chrome-themed kitchen, which was about 8 feet by 8, lined with cupboards and appliances on each side. Maddie hung nervously in the doorway, looking down at her feet. *What the hell am I doing here?* she thought. *This is crazy.* Summer turned to look at Maddie. Maddie looked up and their gazes locked.

"Are you okay, Maddie?" Summer asked.

"Yes," she replied anxiously.

They stared at each other in silence for a few seconds before Maddie began to walk forward towards Summer. Her steps were slow but confident. She could feel the pull of Summer like a magnet, drawing her closer. Their eyes never wavered from each other. Maddie stopped when she was about half a foot away from Summer. She could smell the sweet and fruity fragrance of Summer's perfume and feel the warmth of her breath. She reached forward with her right hand and touched the side of Summer's face. They had been in silence for some time now. The only thing in the air was the tension between them. It was magnetic: a strong force working its unrelenting influence on them. Nothing could stop what was about to happen—it was the work of forces beyond comprehension. Summer's eyes were filled with excitement and longing and Maddie wondered what hers looked like to Summer. Butterflies were using her stomach as a punching bag, flying around so fast it felt as though they'd burst out. Her nerves and every part of her body were on high alert, her breathing fast and heavy. Maddie could take no more. With her other hand she gently pulled Summer closer to her and touched Summer's lips slightly with her own in a movement that was both timid and unstoppable.

Summer responded instantly, taking Maddie in her arms and bringing their bodies even tighter. Their lips were pressed firmly together in a passionate embrace full of lust, longing and magnetism. The moment took Maddie's breath away—her head was spinning and her mind filled with happiness and light. Summer's soft lips moved in unison with Maddie's, working as a team to communicate their chemistry and connection in a way impossible with words. The kiss ended and the women moved back from each other slightly. Maddie looked in awe at Summer.

"Wow," Summer said with a smile.

"Wow," Maddie agreed.

"I didn't know you could do that to me," Summer commented.

"I didn't know I could do that," Maddie said with a playful smile.

"That's been coming ever since I laid eyes on you," Summer remarked.

"You're right. I want to do it again. But it's wrong. I shouldn't be doing this, Summer. But it just feels like I can't fight it, like forces are pulling us together."

"I know what you mean. There is a connection I never thought I'd find," Summer said softly.

"I don't know what this means. All I know is that ever since I met you, you've been on my mind. I haven't had the nightmares since I met you. I was filled with darkness every night, but you are like a ray of light."

"I feel it too, Maddie," Summer replied with a charismatic smile.

She moved forward and kissed Maddie, meeting her lips with a soft and passionate kiss, stealing Maddie's breath. They parted again, and Maddie smiled at Summer, attraction and yearning in her eyes.

"I can't ignore this, Summer. I need to figure out what this is, what this means and what to do next. It's really confusing."

"I know. I know you have Jeremy and Jamie to think about. I know this is wrong, but I want you, Maddie."

"I want you too, Summer. I want to see what we can have here. It's the first time in years I've felt excited and truly alive," Maddie smiled.

Summer pulled Maddie close in a caring embrace. Maddie smiled. This was the biggest shock of her life, but it made sense. Summer was the missing piece.

SECRETS OF THE HEART

by

Liz Kerr

Liz is Australian but has spent the past twelve years living on the small but beautiful British island of Guernsey. She shares a home with her gorgeous 'wife' of twelve years, three lively dogs and a lazy cat, splitting her time between working as a photographer and finance tutor. Knee injuries have meant Liz is now able to dedicate more time to writing and is a sucker for a good love story.

Chapter 1

"'Ands above your 'ead where I can see 'em!" Fanny starts at the harshly spoken words, fearful eyes fixed on the tall, stocky man astride a large, black horse prancing on the dusty road beside their wooden wagon. He lifts his right arm, pointing a revolver straight at Fanny, who swallows, eyes narrowing until the black metal is all she can see. Her mother screams loudly on the seat next to her and the gun wavers between the two women.

"Shut up!" The rough voice is muffled behind the scarf hiding the bushranger's face, only his eye sockets visible as he stares unblinkingly at Fanny, who shivers in fear. A wide-brimmed hat hides the top half of the man's face, and Fanny wrenches her gaze away to face her mother, whose hands are clutched in her lap, shaking uncontrollably.

"Mama, shhh—we don't want to get shot," Fanny begs, covering the older woman's mouth with her small gloved hand. Her mother whimpers once and nods, closing her eyes and leaning back in her seat as she buries her face in her hands.

"And over your coin and jewellery," the man demands, his horse fidgeting as he edges closer, raising the gun again.

"Please don't—it's all we've got to start our new life in the colony," Fanny's father pleads, hands wrapped tightly around the reins of the two horses standing patiently in the middle of the narrow road. Fanny trembles as her eyes dart around the forest around them: dark green trees crowding in, tall branches meeting overhead, blocking the bright afternoon sun. The cool air is a welcome relief after the heat of the open road, the fresh minty smell of the trees filling Fanny's nostrils as she breathes deeply.

"That's not me problem now, 'and it over." The man holds a filthy hand out and Fanny recoils as the bushranger's rotten breath hits her in the face, the scarf doing nothing to mask the stench.

"Hiyee!" The bushranger's head snaps up at the shout ringing out from behind them, the sound of a galloping horse approaching. The man wheels away, thundering off down the narrow dirt track and quickly disappearing from view amongst the thick trees.

*

The stranger pulls his bay horse up next to the Wilsons' wagon, his horse panting heavily.

"Are you all right? Did he get anything?" The man's clean-shaven face is mostly hidden by a wide-brimmed hat, dark brown and dusty like the bushranger's, smooth cheeks flushed from the exertion.

"He didn't get anything, thanks to you," Fanny's Papa says, slumping back in his seat. Fanny turns to her mother, who has collapsed against her, sobbing quietly into her handkerchief. She puts her arm around the small woman, squeezing her narrow shoulders in comfort.

"Thank you for saving us, sir." The man laughs heartily at Fanny's words, leaning back on his horse as it dances in a circle.

"Think nothing of it. I'd advise you to avoid travelling at night, as there are some nasty characters around." The man peers under the brim of his hat and Fanny's heart beats faster as bright blue eyes bore into hers, winking slyly.

"G'day to you." Without another word, the lithe man touches his hat in salute, galloping off in the same direction as the bushranger.

Fanny lets out the breath she'd been holding, fanning her face with her hand as she stares after the retreating figure, heart still thumping loudly in her chest, and thoughts of the handsome man's cheeky wink bringing a blush to her face.

*

The Wilsons reach Blackheath, in the heart of the Blue Mountains, several days later, with no further incident. The talk around town is full of stories about gangs of bushrangers roaming outside the settlements, holding up wagons as people make the thirty-mile journey west from Sydney to the newly-discovered inland area. Fanny's thoughts return often to the day they were held up and saved by the stranger. She tries to remember everything she can about the handsome man with the laughing blue eyes and smooth tanned skin, wishing he'd taken off his hat so she could have seen his whole face.

Twenty-year-old Fanny trudges up the steep main road on her way to the grocery store, thankful her parents finally let her wander unaccompanied now they're in Australia. The midday sun burns through her dress and sweat drips down her back. She's thankful for the bonnet protecting her fair skin, the heat more uncomfortable than anything she's experienced. The young lass is so lost in her thoughts, she doesn't notice the shadow stop in her path.

"Oh!" Fanny exclaims, head snapping back as she smacks into the tall figure. "I'm sorry." She fingers her tender lip and squints upwards, noticing a tall person wearing a wide hat, before recognising the sparkling eyes. "You!" Fanny exclaims. The man in front of her was the one who had saved them a month before. He is tall, with Fanny only reaching to his chin, and his skin is a golden teak colour, as if he spends most of his time outdoors in the sun.

"Good afternoon." The man lifts his hat slightly, bowing in greeting.

"What are you doing here?" Fanny asks, stepping in beside him as they continue the journey up the hill.

"I live nearby." The man's full lips curve upwards in a grin as he nods back down the hill.

"I... I'm Fanny. Fanny Wilson." Fanny stutters over the words, suddenly nervous, knowing her mother wouldn't approve her being out in public without a chaperone.

"I know."

"You do?" Fanny asks in astonishment, gaping at the man she guesses to be five years older than herself.

"Yes. We don't get many handsome single lasses moving to Blackheath." Fanny blushes at the words and moves faster, the man's longer legs easily keeping up. "I'm sorry if I embarrassed you." He apologises after a few moments' silence, having noticed Fanny's eyes fixed on the ground, jaw clenching as she grinds her teeth.

"That's all right. I... I... I'm not used to it is all." Fanny kicks at the dust with her shoe, a cloud flying up and making her cough.

"We'll have to change that, won't we, Miss Wilson?" They've reached the small store and Fanny waits while the man opens the door, holding it so she can pass through. She sidles past into the dim room, tensing as her arm brushes his chest, the faint smell of horses and sweat not unpleasant.

"I'd like that," Fanny replies shyly, blushing again as he gazes at her intently, before nodding.

"Miss Wilson? My name's Charlie Thomas." He speaks quietly as the door closes between them, leaving her alone in the cool room.

*

"Mama, guess who I ran into at the store today?" Fanny is breathless after rushing back down the hill laden down with shopping, excited about sharing the news with her mother.

"I didn't know you knew anyone here yet." Fanny's mother sits at the kitchen table chopping vegetables for their supper, glancing briefly at her daughter before turning her attention back to the potatoes.

"Charlie Thomas—the man who rescued us from the bushrangers. He knew my name." Fanny's hazel eyes sparkle with excitement as she shifts from one foot to another, hands waving as she talks.

"Be careful, Fanny—a man like that is only after one thing."

"Oh, Mama, he's not like that at all. He's quite the gentleman." Fanny picks up a piece of potato and slips it in her mouth, her mother slapping her hand away with irritation.

"Mmmhmm, well, I want you to be careful all the same."

*

"Good afternoon, Miss Wilson." Fanny jumps at the low voice behind her, hand going to her throat in surprise. It's a week since she's seen Charlie, and he's as dashing as she remembers, straight teeth white against his tan.

"Mr Thomas," she says shyly, eyes fixed on her feet instead of the man in front of her. She folds her arms across her middle, worried her dress is too worn, as she's had it since she was still in England.

"Please, call me Charlie. May I escort you to your destination?" Charlie's head is tilted sideways, the upper part of his face hidden by the ever-present hat.

"I don't actually have a destination," Fanny confesses, her eyes travelling briefly up his long body to his narrow face.

"Then may I have the pleasure of your company in your wanderings around town? I can protect you from any criminals." Charlie winks, and Fanny throws her head back, laughing at his words.

"What if you're a criminal?"

"I would have thought my reputation was beyond reproach—I did save you from one of them, after all."

"Ah yes, you did. Unless you were trying to trick me into thinking you weren't a criminal." Charlie glances away for a moment before gazing curiously at Fanny, a frown appearing on his boyish face.

"No, Miss Wilson, I wouldn't ever try to trick you."

"I believe you," Fanny says softly, wondering at the shadows in Charlie's eyes. "Tell me Charlie, do you have an occupation?" The two set off back down the hill, ambling side-by-side in the early afternoon, Fanny squinting against the bright sunlight bouncing off the ground and into her eyes.

"I'm a dairy farmer." Fanny's heart skips a beat as one side of Charlie's mouth curls into a smile when he glances sideways at her.

"I don't want to keep you from your work. I'm sure there's a lot you should be doing."

"I work enough as it is—an hour off isn't going to make any difference, and my workers make sure the chores are all done. It's not often I get to enjoy such a lovely day." Charlie strolls with his hands behind his back, shirt stretched tight over wiry shoulders, thick boots quiet on the dusty ground that hasn't seen rain for many weeks.

"Do you often save families getting held up by bushrangers?" Fanny asks, a teasing note in her voice.

"No, you're the first," Charlie answers, a broad grin making him seem younger than Fanny first thought.

"Thank you—you don't realise how much it would have ruined us, having everything stolen before we even arrived. Ma and Pa had saved for years in England to make the journey and gave up everything to come to Australia."

"I know how much it would have affected me when I first arrived, so I have some idea. I'm just happy I rode up at the right time."

"So am I," Fanny replies, thinking she's happy in more ways than one.

*

The pair lapse into a comfortable silence as they stroll down the road, turning left onto a different road.

"Where are we going?" Fanny asks curiously, not having explored the local area yet.

"Patience, Miss Wilson, you'll soon see," Charlie teases, smiling gently at the lass at his side, chestnut hair curling midway down her back, hazel eyes light in the sunshine. Fanny's narrow waist flares out slightly at her hips, her plain brown dress hugging her curves nicely.

"It's so different from England," Fanny glances around at the scenery. "Trees, birds—even the smells are different."

"It's true," Charlie agrees, following her gaze to the tall eucalyptuses lining the road, shedding bark in great sheets. The trees' scent surrounds them, the freshness contrasting with the heaviness of the hot summer air.

"Sometimes in the mornings a blue mist hangs over the valley from the eucalyptus trees. I've never seen anything like it." Charlie's voice is wistful as his gaze turns inwards.

"Is that what those trees are? Eucalyptus?" Fanny points to one of the trees towering high overhead. "I want to know everything there is to know about this country. Will you teach me?"

*

Fanny and Charlie meet every few days for the next month as Charlie teaches her everything he knows about the country and they explore the area. Today they stand at a lookout over a deep canyon covered in trees, a waterfall flowing down the cliff face further along the valley. Fanny stands in rapt attention as Charlie points out landmarks, teaching her the names of the birds flying overhead. She learns about the noisy squawking cockatoos with yellow combs on their heads gliding by and the kookaburras that Fanny is yet to see, their maniacal laughter echoing across the canyon.

"You've taught me so much—thank you, Charlie," Fanny enthuses as they climb the hill to her house, the sun casting long shadows as it dips low in the sky. She watches the quiet man next to her, heart beating quickly as the heat from his body spreads into her. Fanny often catches Charlie gazing at her wistfully and she wishes he'd just take her in his arms and kiss her, the thought often keeping her up at night.

"It's my pleasure, Miss Wilson: I enjoy teaching you," Charlie replies, hat still pulled low over his eyes.

"Please, call me Fanny," Fanny asks, not for the first time. "I was wondering… " She takes a deep breath and stops walking, facing the taller man who stands patiently, waiting for her to finish her sentence. "Ma's asked if you would come around for afternoon tea next week. She would like to thank you for saving us."

"I… I…" The usually confident Charlie is hesitant, wringing his hands together and shifting his weight from one foot to the other. "I don't usually go to other people's houses. I ah… I'm not very good with people." He meets Fanny's eyes, his expression hardening and she resists the urge to take his hand.

"Nonsense, you are very good at talking to me. Please, Charlie? Would you do it for me?" Charlie's face softens at the hope in Fanny's eyes, her eyebrows raised in question.

"Very well, Fanny—for you," he sighs, knowing Fanny is the first woman he's met who he can't say no to, also understanding how much trouble she could make for him.

Chapter 2

Fanny jumps up at the knock on the front door after sitting in the airy front room all morning, unable to concentrate. She rushes to the door and yanks it open, smiling when she sees Charlie wearing a clean blue cotton shirt and black trousers, his thick boots shined and gleaming.

"Charlie! Come in." Fanny opens the door wider and gestures with her head, the smell of baking bread wafting out from the kitchen.

"Miss Wilson." Charlie bows, straightening, and taking his hat off for the first time. Fanny swallows a gasp as light blue eyes framed by long eyelashes capture hers. Charlie's hair is so dark it's almost black, swept back from his face and cut short around his ears to just above his slender neck. Fanny jerks as their fingers touch when she takes his hat, lifting her head to see Charlie's expressive eyes shining back at her.

"Come in and meet my mother."

*

The afternoon drags for Charlie, sitting in the uncomfortable chair drinking tea, trying his best to not seem like the common dairy farmer he is. He wants Fanny to be proud of him, and glances over to her, warm eyes glowing back at him, accompanied by the dimpled smile he'd do anything to see. He takes a deep breath, knowing he has to stop seeing Fanny before the affection he feels for her grows any more, the thought already almost more than he can bear.

"Mrs Wilson, thank you for a lovely afternoon, but I must be getting back to the farm."

"Of course, Mr Thomas, thank you for visiting, and you must call again soon."

"I will," Charlie lies, standing and turning to Fanny, who sits waiting in her wooden chair, hands clenched tightly in her lap.

"It was nice to see you again, Miss Wilson."

"And you." Fanny doesn't meet Charlie's eyes and without another word he makes his way to the front door, letting himself out quietly and taking the porch steps two at a time.

"Charlie!" He stops twenty feet away and slowly turns. Fanny stands hidden in the shadows at the front door and takes a tentative step towards him, their eyes locked, as she slowly climbs down the stairs, stopping a foot away.

"Fanny..." Charlie doesn't know what to say, the distraught expression on the lass's face bringing a lump to his throat that he swallows painfully.

"You're not coming back, are you?" Her eyes brim with tears as her mouth quivers, folding her arms across her chest protectively.

"I can't... I already have feelings for you and I just... I can't."

"Why not?" Fanny closes her eyes, and when she opens them again a single tear escapes down her cheek.

"Fanny..." Charlie says softly, reaching out a gentle hand to wipe it away. "I care. I care too much and it's not fair to mislead you in any way. I'm sorry if I already have."

"You've never misled me, I'd just hoped..." Fanny sniffles, and Charlie hands her his clean handkerchief.

"If things were different, or in a different, life maybe… maybe we could be together, but we can't." Charlie rests his hand for a moment on Fanny's cheek, leaning forward and kissing her forehead gently, warm lips resting a moment before he pulls away reluctantly.

"Not even if I know?" Fanny peers up at him through her tears, eyes pleading with Charlie.

"Know?" Charlie freezes, his heart suddenly pounding so loud in his chest, he's worried Fanny might hear it.

"Know you are a woman." The breath rushes out of Charlie's chest and he stumbles back in shock, out of touching range of Fanny. "Please, Charlie, don't go, talk to me." Charlie stares back in terror, wide eyes reflecting the fear he's lived with for years. He shakes his head and pivots, tearing up the road and away from the woman who has the power to destroy him.

Fanny watches the scared man take off, her heart going out him. She finally realised what was so different about Charlie when he took his hat off and she saw his face. His features are much too fine for a man: soft, full red lips and smooth skin, obviously a woman's if you look closely enough, even though he's tall and muscular after spending most of his time outside working. Fanny wants to chase Charlie and tell him everything will be all right, but she's not sure if she would be lying. She's already halfway in love with Charlie, thinking about him constantly, his smile making her heart skip a beat and his nearness making her a little dizzy. She trudges despondently back inside to her room at the back of the house, flopping on to her bed and spending the rest of the night deciding what she's going to do.

*

Fanny plods up the now familiar hill, thoughts turned inwards, as she ignores her surroundings. It's been two weeks since Charlie ran off, and Fanny's spent most of her waking hours thinking about him and the truth she's discovered. She watches out for the familiar figure every time she goes to the grocery store, but he stays away, and she realises it's unlikely she'll see the man again. Her heart aches for what might have been as she tries to convince herself she didn't have feelings for the dairy farmer, her heart not listening to what her head tells her.

Charlie spends his time working with his men and tending to his farm—milking, watering and feeding the cows. He works until late, often collapsing into bed too exhausted to think about Fanny. Much. Charlie lies on his back staring at the ceiling, pictures of Fanny running through his head. Memories of her laughing at something or gasping in wonder at the valley spread before her making him smile. Charlie's heart grows heavy with missing the lass—even though he'd only known her a short time, she's been able to get inside his barren heart. Eventually, he falls into a fitful sleep fully clothed, dreams of Fanny's sweetness and innocence mixed with nightmares of an angry mob chasing him, trying to shoot him down as he desperately attempts to escape.

Bang, bang, bang! Charlie bolts upright in bed, breathing heavily, eyes wide with fear as they dart around his bare bedroom, the first hint of daylight sneaking in the wide window. He's normally up by now, but has taken the day off to gather his thoughts. The bang comes again and he leaps out of bed, rushing to the kitchen as he tucks his shirt in, picking up his rifle and padding cautiously to the front door. He stands to the side of the door with the rifle pointed at the floor, heart pounding in his chest.

"Who is it?" Charlie calls out tentatively, rifle resting loosely in his arms.

"Charlie? I need to talk to you!" Charlie's mouth drops open at the desperate voice, muffled through the door.

"Fanny?" Charlie carefully rests the gun down against the wall and opens the door, Fanny standing forlornly on the other side, hair hidden by a bonnet, a plain green dress covering most of her arms and legs. "Come in." Charlie opens the door wider so Fanny can enter. "What are you doing here?" he asks belatedly, moving into the kitchen as Fanny removes her bonnet and trails after him, eyes darting around the large house with its dark wood floor and bare white walls.

"We need to talk," Fanny says standing at the door, unsure of her welcome.

"Do you want some coffee?" Charlie asks, tilting his head towards the stove.

"Yes, please," The two remain silent as Charlie moves efficiently around the space, a few minutes later bringing the mugs to the scarred wooden kitchen table, pulling out a chair and inviting Fanny to sit, before moving to another chair.

"Charlie, I want to apologise for what I said. It's been on my mind ever since and I need to talk about it." Fanny watches Charlie earnestly, but his face is averted as he stares out the kitchen window, both hands curled around his full coffee cup.

"There's nothing to apologise for, Fanny, let's just forget it happened." Charlie's voice is hoarse and Fanny sees his hands trembling.

"But, you see, I don't want to," Fanny whispers, climbing out of her chair to move around the table to stand in front of Charlie, forcing him to look up at her.

"Charlie, I want... I want to be with you." Fanny holds her breath as emotion flits across Charlie's face, hope soon eclipsed by despair.

"Fanny, you know I can't," Charlie swallows, and tears his eyes away, his finger tracing one of the scratches on the table over and over.

"Tell me you don't have feelings for me," Fanny demands, voice rough with emotion.

"I... I..." Charlie makes the mistake of lifting his head, seeing hot tears in Fanny's eyes as she waits expectantly. "Oh hell." Charlie jumps out of his seat, making Fanny step back in surprise. He grabs her around the waist and kisses her roughly, pulling her body to his. Fanny only hesitates a moment before she throws her arms around Charlie's neck, kissing him back passionately. Fanny groans as Charlie's hot mouth moves over her face, kissing the tears away and covering every inch of skin, finally moving back to claim her waiting lips. "Oh Fanny. I'm sorry—I didn't mean to do that," Charlie apologises after breaking the kiss, and leans back to gaze into eyes sparkling with emotion.

"I did," Fanny laughs as she goes back for another heated kiss, Charlie's mouth opening under the assault, his tongue tentatively making its way into Fanny's mouth. Fanny cleaves to Charlie, her hand behind his head pulling him down. Charlie finally pulls away again, eyes shining with emotion, squeezing Fanny in a tight hug.

"What about…" He takes a deep breath, squaring his shoulders unconsciously and gazing down at the young lass in his arms. "What about me being a… a woman?" He shudders, eyes too scared to look directly at Fanny.

"I love you, Charlie. That means I love everything about you." Fanny's voice is soft but sure. "I've never lain with anyone before, so I'm not sure exactly what it means, but I want to know all of you. The way you look at me makes my heart beat loud in my chest and my knees go weak. Fanny rests her head on Charlie's chest, the steady thumping of his heart reassuring as she squeezes her arms around his narrow waist. They stay unmoving for so long that Fanny eventually tilts her head to meet Charlie's eyes, tears running unheeded down his face. "Oh, sweetheart," Fanny says, pulling out of Charlie's embrace and grabbing his hand, pulling him towards the door at the back of the room. "Take me to your bedroom." Charlie obeys numbly, wiping the tears away impatiently and clinging onto Fanny's small hand as they move silently through the house, the only noise their footsteps on the wooden floor.

*

Charlie stops at the doorway to his bedroom, turning to face Fanny, eyes full of fear.

"I've never done this before," he whispers, clutching Fanny's hand in his rough calloused palm.

"Neither have I, but we'll work it out together," Fanny replies, stepping up close and resting her hand on Charlie's chest, reaching up to kiss him gently on the mouth. The kiss turns hungry and Charlie wraps both arms around Fanny, crushing her to him. He walks them to the bed and collapses onto it, pulling the girl down with him and rolling her on to her back. Soft hands move Fanny's hair out of the way, Charlie kissing exposed skin as she tilts her head back, eyes closed at the soft touch. Warm lips move down her neck to the top of her dress, Fanny arching off the bed, searching for the touch, hands clutching the bedcovers. She whimpers and opens her eyes to see blue eyes shining with love as long fingers unbutton her green dress, each snick making Fanny's chest heave with desire until soon she lies naked, cool air puckering her nipples.

"Charlie, please, can I?" Fanny asks softly, her hands pulling at his white shirt, tugging it out of Charlie's trousers as she reaches up and kisses her lover's chin.

"I... I don't know." Charlie's eyes close for a moment and he draws a sharp breath as Fanny's small hand sneaks underneath to stroke the bare skin of his belly.

"I want to see you. All of you." Charlie finally nods, and Fanny kneels opposite him, gently unbuttoning his shirt and stopping for a kiss every few seconds. Finally the shirt drops off Charlie's shoulders, exposing a flat stomach, leaving only a bandage wrapped around his chest. Fanny takes the end of the material gently and unwinds it from Charlie's still body, dropping it off the side of the bed as Charlie's small breasts are exposed to Fanny's fiery gaze. She pushes him back on the bed and straddles him, her hungry mouth moving over his stomach and chest, kissing her way up and down his body as his hands caress her back.

"You're so handsome," Fanny whispers, their hands moving together to remove the rest of Charlie's clothes, the change from man to woman complete. Fanny climbs on top of Charlie and entwines their legs, breasts pressed together as they lie naked, touching everywhere possible. Charlie lifts Fanny up her body, her demanding mouth replacing the hands exploring Fanny's breasts.

"Oh!" Fanny exclaims, every touch making her think her skin's going to catch fire. She gasps as a flood of moisture coats her leg, nestled between Charlie's legs, their bodies moving together rhythmically, uneven breaths the only noise as impatient hands move frantically across long stretches of skin.

"Charlie, touch me please—touch me before I die," Fanny pleads, holding her breath as Charlie's hand moves slowly down her body to between her legs, shouting out in pleasure as slender fingers caress her before sliding inside. Fanny's eyes slam shut and she moves in time with the skilful fingers playing her, tension building deep inside until she's worried she might explode. Fanny tenses as the fingers move even faster, every muscle in her body clenching before she cries out one last time, shuddering and sinking back to the bed, unable to move.

"Uhhh. I'm speechless," Fanny says a few minutes later, opening her eyes to see Charlie lying on her side, the backs of her fingers trailing down Fanny's naked body from her shoulder to her hip and up again.

"That's a first," Charlie teases, leaning forward for a kiss.

"Thank you for letting me undress you. I know how hard that must have been." Fanny brushes her thumb over Charlie's full lips, her eyes soft with desire. "You are so handsome." Charlie searches Fanny's eyes, his own baring his soul.

"Please don't leave me, Fanny, I couldn't survive it if you did—I've let you in so far already."

"I'm not leaving you, Charlie. I want to be with you for as long as you'll have me," Fanny reassures Charlie as she leans over the other woman, kissing her deeply before pulling back and gazing deeply into dark blue eyes. "But there is one thing I want right now." Charlie baulks at the glint in Fanny's eyes as she's pushed back on the bed, Fanny hovering over her with arms braced on either side of Charlie's body.

"You can have anything you want."

"I want to take you and make you mine," Fanny's hand moves down Charlie's body to the moisture pooling between her legs, claiming Charlie completely and leaving no doubt about exactly what she wants.

INHERITANCE

by

Helen Larder

Helen Larder graduated from the M.A. Novel Writing course at Manchester Metropolitan University and her first novel, 'Treasure', was published by Diva Press in 2003. The narrative is contained within the time frame of one weekend, as the characters become involved in a car treasure hunt.

Her second novel, 'Anarchy' published in 2008, was inspired by twenty-five years experience, teaching young people in the inner city. It is aimed at a teenage audience and intended to reflect young people's lives in a realistic and thought provoking way.

Currently, she is completing her third novel, a thriller, called 'Chaos' which follows 5 sixteen year olds, investigating a murder and a corrupt politician.

She has taught postgraduate, undergraduate and F.E. students, lecturing in creative writing, script writing and acting.

Helen Larder was born in Yorkshire in 1958 and now lives in the High Peaks, with her civil partner and their daughter.

"*Last week can-cer ate your Mum, and now your wo-man's leaving.*"

The voice is chanting to the tune of a Christmas carol. Merrily on high.

"*What's next, Jody?*" it sneers. "*Things always come in threes.*"

I've got to make it stop.

"*Shut* the *fuck* up."

A chair scrapes.

Everyone in the café's staring at the head case swearing to herself. Staring at me. Watching me mashing tomatoes into sauce on my plate. Strange—I don't give a damn.

A man gets up from the next table and goes to speak to the woman behind the counter. In the queue, a doll-sized girl yanks her mother's jacket. Makes her bend down, so she can whisper in her ear. *About me.* My fork works faster, turning my food into a bloodbath, splattering the floor. Through my fingers, I can see a plump body heading my way. Ginger hair. Blue-and-white-striped apron. Her hand reaches for the red mess.

"Have you finished with this?"

She can't make me move.

"Not yet."

She hesitates, wondering how to get me out, then gives up, and starts collecting dishes from more reasonable customers.

Someone drops a copy of the "Metro News" on the corner of my table as they leave. When I turn it over, a few grains of rice back up into my mouth. There's a full page photo from the Paris catwalks. A model, her skin the colour of Vaseline, clutching a naked baby like it's a chubby brown parcel. *Brown is the new black.* Its fists are clenched and its eyes fixed on the model's detached expression. Food urges against my throat again, tasting sour the second time around. In my mind, a serrated-edged print of me and Mum superimposes itself over the newspaper, and I see that the newsprint figures are an exact black and white negative of us. Mum even has the same oblivious face as the model. That could've been lack of sleep. No. Trauma, I guess, at the sight of a white baby in her arms...

*

"Mum, what's jungle fever?" I had more questions than most six-year-olds.

Her knife stopped slicing raw chicken.

"*Why*? Who said that?" I didn't want to carry on. "*Who*?"

"Some boys in Miss Adams' class."

Mum laid the knife in the sink, slowly.

"What did they say?"

I wished I'd never asked.

"Something about… an old perv must've caught jungle fever and given you one, to get an ugly monster like me."

"I'm going up to that school, *right now*." She hauled her bobbled cardigan off.

"No. Please." *They'll only do it more.* I leaned my head into her stomach to stop her getting past. Breathed in her coconut scent. "Just tell me what it means."

"Don't you listen to those *liars*, Jody Osango." Her hands cradled my head. "Boys like them just get frightened. They're angry 'cos they never gonna have a chance with a girl as beautiful as you…"

*

Christ. I miss her. I want my Mum. My Marcie. Now I've got no one. No one to stop me being invisible. Need to get out of here, before the crazy stuff takes hold. Stranglehold. I blink away hypodermic tears. Trying to focus. I stand up, shifting my plate, so it doesn't touch my jeans. Got to get away. Somewhere. Anywhere...

*

"*Oh! St-op the bu-s, sto-o-op the bu-us.*"

This is the place.

The carol singer's screeching at the driver, *joy-ful and tri-um-phant*. I don't know where the hell I am.

The deaf bastard doesn't take his eyes off the road. Then I remember, no one else can hear the mad bitch in my head, so I ring the bell. We carry on lurching forward.

I touch his arm.

"Can you let me off here?"

He still doesn't respond.

A river and a post office with a "For Sale" sign fly by as he steers round the corner. Blood pulses hard in my chest. *I'm going to buy that place.*

"*Running away won't help*," my Mother reminds me.

"*A change is as good as a rest*," Gran contradicts her.

When the driver stops at a bus shelter in front of the village pub, I fling myself down the steps, on to a steep grass verge. Haven't got a clue where this place is. Somewhere in the Lakes. Two trains. One bus. Without reading any signposts. *A magical mystery tour.*

I can't see the post office yet, but it's screening on a continuous loop at the back of my eyes. The terraced garden. The path leading to a pebble beach along the riverbank.

I'll sell my place and move here. Never liked that flat anyway. Too cold. Too empty. Too many open-plan lakes of polished floorboards, suspended over the city. I can't even stand within six feet of all that floor-to-ceiling plate-glass without getting vertigo. I shouldn't have let Shelley choose it. Never should have moved in with her…

*

"You'll settle here soon, stop worrying." Shelly positions a square vase of pale lilies at the dead centre of the Perspex table. *She's big. She's everywhere.* "It'll be all right."

I mustn't answer. Anything I say will give her false hope. Can't talk myself into wanting her.

"*Look*, Jody, whatever's bothering you, we can sort it out." Shelly sounds so sure. She's used to telling me my own mind. I refuse to look at her but I can feel she's too close. Too blonde. Too fleshy.

"*A-way in-to dan-ger.*" The carol singing's started again. "*No-o rib for her bed.*"

Eight months is too long to have to listen to Christmas carols. Eight months since all the shops were playing the same tunes. Eight months since Mum started chemo. Eight months since I stopped telling Shelley anything.

"If you'd just *talk* to me," Shelley whines.

My gaze drifts into the bell of one waxy, cream flower. Freezing her out... It was the only way to get rid of her.

*

I balance on the grassy slope as a tractor makes its raucous progress past. Behind it, I can see the post office with its "For Sale" sign.

A bell above the door rings when I push it open. The shop's deserted. Anyone could just walk in and steal everything. Except there's nothing much to take: only a wooden rack of chocolate bars and penny sweets and shelves of dusty, pastel greetings cards. Looks like the rest of the stock is inside that pile of cardboard boxes. *I could do something with this place.* Restore it. Most of the fittings are original. I could buy some interesting gifts for the tourists. Keep essentials for the locals. Drag it into the twenty-first century. If there's an offer in already, I'll up it. Start a bidding war.

In another room, someone's on the phone.

"Have a biscuit, Mum. I'll be there in five minutes." I can hear the woman talking is genuinely patient. "I'll bring a tin of salmon." Her throat sounds raw.

When she walks in and hangs up the phone, she won't meet my eyes. Her grey V-neck sweater and skirt look like a school uniform bought two sizes too big. With her slight frame, sharp features and ponytail, she could be twenty or fifty. As I get nearer, the dry lines at the edges of her eyes say she's nearer my upper estimate. Listlessly, she slides a pile of forms into a worn brown envelope and lets it fall next to a bin bag on the floor.

I clear my throat to make her look at me.

"Am I too late?"

The bridge of her nose pinches into a frown.

"Is it sold already?"

She shakes her head and passes an estate agent's leaflet over the counter. The photo of the post office is nowhere near as compelling as the real thing.

I hold out my hand for her to shake.

"I'm Jody."

She hesitates, presses her lips together, then offers me her fingertips. Her skin's even paler than mine.

"Sorry," I say. "What's your name?"

"Wilshaw."

I smile.

"Do people call you by your surname?" She bows her head, exposing the nape of her neck.

"Jane."

"*Pla-i-n Jane.*" My carol singer begins a new version of Silent Night. "*Ho-l-y Jane. All is harm. All is tight. You're ex-qui-site, n-o mis-take.*"

She unhooks a bunch of keys from the door.

"I've got to go now. Maybe…"

"I've come a long way. I wonder if you could show me around? I won't get another chance to come back."

"*How- still- w-e- see- thee- lie.*" Even though she's a maniac, this time the singer's right: I *am* a liar. The truth is, I don't know how I'll ever leave this place. Whatever else happens, I've got to shake this girl awake. Squeeze her back to life.

"Just a quick look?"

"My mother…"

I try my best smile.

"I'll only be a minute."

She pauses, then pushes the oak door wide and waits. Just stands there.

The interior bears no relation to Jane's grey clothes. I'm confused by a cottage garden of colour. A slant of sunlight warms the fruit and flowers that are painted, printed and sewn on every surface. Silk tangerines and vermilion petals uncurl along a tapestry draped over the table. Gold and jade leaves twine through the rug. Apples and pears swell on the plump cushions. A jar of ceramic asparagus grows beside some real, yellow tea roses—the same ones that frame the window outside. It's a wild orchard room, and

I want it. But when I imagine it stripped of her things, something sore clenches my throat.

Jane shifts. A strand of hair slips from behind her ear. A blush flushes her cheeks. *All this is going to be mine.* I lean forward and press my mouth to her neck. She stiffens. A citrus scent comes off her. It's too late now. I can't back off, even if she's scared. I step close enough to feel the rough, washed-up nylon of her jumper, insinuating my thigh between her legs. As I open my lips over her collarbone, her head tilts back. I can't tell if she likes it, or if she's turning her face out of reach. Sharp pain drags my cunt in a tug of war. Never had rope burns this bad. Need to grind into her. Got to find somewhere solid to crush against her. Grasping her arms, I steer her away from the door and position her in front of the wall. My nails extend into claws, digging in so she can't get away…

"This is the living room. It's small." Jane sounds dismissive, as if she's opposing a poor investment. She hasn't moved. She's still hovering half in and half out of the doorway.

I cover my cheeks with my palms, so she doesn't see them barbecue. So she can't guess what I've been thinking.

"It's fine." I point towards the stairs. "How many bedrooms?"

"Look." She's changing her mind. "I've got to get over to my mother's."

Stall her.

"What about the account books? Have you been making enough to live on?"

She clasps her fingers together, begging.

"She's not well."

"I'm sorry… really. I'm not usually so…"

Follow her.

"Does your mum live in the village?"

She nods.

"Maybe I could walk with you, to save time, so you can tell me a bit about the place."

She grows still, then grabs a tin of salmon from the sideboard.

"All right."

*

I watch the muscles work in Jane's forearms as she slices the sandwich. White bread.

"Couldn't you persuade your Mum to move into the post office with you?"

She glances at me as if I should know better, then picks up the plate. On the mantelpiece, a two-year-old version of Jane stumbles towards her mother. Smiling. When she's halfway up the stairs, I tag along behind her. Maybe the mother has got a say in the sale of the property. Better keep her sweet.

"Can I go in and say hello?"

Jane stops abruptly. I can tell her patience is worn ragged.

"What's the *matter* with you? My mum's had a fall... a stroke. She's not... right."

I catch up with her as she reaches the landing.

"My mother died a couple of days ago."

How low can you go?

She stares, probing for lies, then sees something in my face that makes her eyes fill and gestures towards the bedroom.

"Mum, this is—"

"I *know* who it is." The old woman slams a hand over her breast as if she's starring in a melodrama, then reaches out to me from the bed. The veins that cover her arms are bloodily purple under her thin skin. "I didn't know if you'd come." She threads her fingers through mine.

"Mum, you haven't met. Jody is interested in buying our—"

"Don't be *silly*." Shaking her head, Jane's mother sees the sandwich. "I can't eat that. I'll have a fruit salad."

"All right." Jane's eyes hold mine, warning me. "Jody, do you want to come and have a cup of tea?"

"No!" The old woman pulls me closer to the source of a faint smell of urine. "Just give us a few minutes. On our own."

"I don't—" Jane protests.

"Go on." Her mother waves her away.

Jane considers us both for a moment before she goes. *Don't leave me with her. Not this again. Sick beds scare me shitless.* Catching me off-guard, her skeletal hands yank so suddenly that I over-balance and sit on the bed.

"I thought you'd never forgive me."

What the hell am I supposed to say to that?

"What's happened to your skin?" She touches my face. "Why are you so pale? You look ill."

I fire off telepathic messages to Jane. *Please come and rescue me.* Through a cloudy glass of water, a set of teeth grimaces at me.

"Remember that first summer you were here?" She doesn't seem to require a reaction, so I keep quiet. "It was so hot that year. We were never inside. Even slept in the garden."

For God's sake; how long does a fruit salad take?

"I used to measure the shade of your skin every week with a liquorice stick. By the time we went back to school, you were nearly the same colour as it. I always went like a lobster and peeled off in strips." There's an urgent change of key. "I've *never* stopped being sorry, you know. It's just that the pair of us stuck out enough as it was, without... I wouldn't say no, if you asked me now." *Who does she think I am?* She fingers my mouth. Without the support of her teeth, her lips cave in. "I've never had it so sweet since." Her hands grasp the back of my neck, forcing my face into hers. As I lurch forward, her mouth sucks mine and before I can pull away, her tongue rolls round inside. I taste cheese. My gagging reflex kicks in and I extricate myself carefully from her damaged arms. Her eyes are spilling. "You haven't forgiven me, have you?"

I pause. What harm can it do?

"Yes. I have."

Her eyelids lower before she lies back on the pillow.

As if she's been listening outside the door, Jane appears and tries to hand a bowl to her mother.

The old woman turns over.

"I can't eat now."

Jane motions me out of the room.

"I'm sorry about that." She sounds like she thinks I brought it on myself.

"There's a drink for you downstairs. I need to get Mum to swallow her tablets."

I'm dismissed.

The cup of tea she's left on the Formica table is floating with greasy cream. Should have told her I take it black.

I'm an intruder. The back door is open, so I wander out into the weeds and the last hint of sun.

I can't steal other people's lives. But I'm not going back to my own. Easing my mobile from my jeans, I switch it on. There won't be any recorded condolences. Haven't told anyone yet. About Mum. About Shelley. The receiver is so tight to my head, it sets off a searing itch in my ear.

"You have two new voice mail messages."

As soon as I hear the name of the funeral directors and the word "arrangements", I skip to the next one.

"Hello." *It's Jane.* I swing round to make sure she's not playing at pantomimes. *She's behind you.* But everything inside the house is quiet. "I'm trying to get in touch with Marcie Osango, on behalf of my mother, Sheila Wilshaw." I can imagine Jane pressing her lips together while she decides what to say. Can almost see her sharp nose, making beak-like investigations into the phone. "They knew each other when Marcie was evacuated to Cumbria. If I've reached the wrong person, my apologies." She takes a breath and enunciates her number clearly.

My mind hurls at the idea of my Mum and the old woman upstairs as a *couple*. Marcie and Sheila lying awake in the hot grass. I can hear water running down the drain from the kitchen. There's no such thing as fate. I must've seen a photo of the post office in one of Mum's albums. Déjà vu. Must've heard her talk about this place. Stored it somewhere at the back of my mind.

Maybe I should bury Mum here.

Mum begins humming, "*Coming for to carry me home.*"

"You used to sing me to sleep with that one," I say out loud. But I don't need to remind her.

A breeze runs through the garden to meet me. I could lean forward and lift off the ground.

I press redial. Inside, the phone starts ringing.

SATIN OVER SAND

by

Sam Paterson-Sleep

Some of her time teaching, some of her time thinking about writing and the rest of her time on Twitter: this is how Sam lives. Every now and then she actually puts pen to paper and writes some words. Food, especially cake, is something she is utterly obsessed by. Her natural habitat is people watching in cafes where she tweets, drinks coffee and eats cake and, hell, if you push her she may admit that she has been thinking about writing. She loves telling stories, and finds her powers of observation to be a massive help when it comes to creating characters. Her teaching is often an outlet for these stories but fortunately, she teaches drama so her students don't mind too much.

Her short story 'Satin Over Sand' is a product of recollecting bad attempts at chatting up women, whilst working behind a bar. Fortunately one of these bad attempts led to Sam meeting her partner whom she has now lived with in Sussex for many years.

Distracting herself from the mundane events that she calls a life by writing stories, Sam pops them on Tumblr every now and then. You can find them at: www.samjpaterson.tumblr.com

You can tweet Sam (@SamJPaterson

She felt the brush of the fingertips on the back of her hand as she passed the drink over. Warm. Soft. Like satin over sand.

A moment flashes between them, a split second of history. Of future. Of now. She felt her skin prickle at the touch. Goosebumps crept up her: unexpected, excited.

Her stomach lurched, reached towards her heart, pounding suddenly in her chest. She felt her blood rush, colour spring to her cheeks. Maybe she shouldn't be giving so much away—too much too soon? Or maybe she should, maybe this was her heart's way of telling her to make a move.

"A move...? Surely it's too soon?"

Her pupils dilate as their eyes meet, blinking she quickly looks down. A smile curls at the corner of her mouth, creeping into her blush. Suddenly shy, she raised a hand and rubbed some imaginary tension away from the back of her neck. She took a breath and looked up, back into those eyes. Those pools of sea-green. Of faraway sunshine. Of lying on beaches, slowly melting in the heat. Melting. Melting into those eyes of sea-green. Time came to a standstill. Corny, but true. She thought of all those films, all those musicals she had seen, where everything slows down, the surrounding world drifts away into a blur of soft focus, leaving only the two protagonists. The *innamorati*. Much too much in love. Unable to touch for fear of the love destroying them. A love so powerful it stops the world. That's what it felt like to her. No fireworks, no crashing orchestrations, no… anything. The tinny bass of the music and the hubbub of the crowd faded into silence. The clamouring for a drink, the hustle at the bar, drifted out of sight. It was just the two of them. Alone. Locked in the touch of fingertips on skin. Satin over sand. Eyes gazing into eyes.

"Is this even real?"

She became aware that something had changed. There had been a shift whilst her time stood still. She blinked, not wanting to break this moment, this power that had taken her over. She blinked again, ears straining to hear. Straining to bring her back to the reality. She looks, beginning to take in more than the eyes, more than the sea green. She starts to notice the face. Her face. Gazing at her. Smiling. Those sea-green eyes, pulling her in again. Those sea-green eyes. Framed by smiling creases. Laughter lines. Deep, well-earned, enjoyed. Her eyes shift away from the sea-green, tugged at by her ears straining to hear. She traces smiling creases down the face, pausing over the smile. That smile. Smiling at her. Those lips, moving the smile. No. Not moving the smile, simply moving. Moving. Making shapes. Speaking.

"You can let go now, if you want."

An awkward moment, the smile now polite, hesitant, uncertain. Those smiling creases fading, lessening as the volume is turned back up. As others come into focus, jostling at the bar, fighting for attention. She stops breathing momentarily, suddenly aware of the situation, of her hand clamped round the glass. A gentle tug as she tries to break it free. The colour that was a shy shade of red now burns bright. Crimson. Embarrassment rings her eyes, fuelled by the stare that has replaced the smile. She releases her grip, but knocks the glass. A wave topples out, washing the contact away. Destroying the satin over sand. Cold. Unwanted. Extinguishing the momentary flame. The burn of love. Powerful, world stopping, love.

"Sorry," she murmurs, breathing out an awkward smile as if to punctuate her apology. Inside she is crying, dying a little. Her heart stopped pounding and started sinking like a stone. Plummets down, deeper than the pit of her stomach which follows in dread and despair. Down it sinks. Down into her boots, through the soles and into the ground below. There it attempts to dig upwards. Dig a hole in the ground. To swallow her up. To bury her embarrassment. To hide her love. Her all-consuming love that started with a touch. Satin over sand.

"Idiot!" her brain screams. *"Idiot. Fucking stupid, dumb-arsed fucking thick-shitted idiot!"*

Her heart scrapes below, caught on the sole of her boot. Stuck underneath the man-made, non-slip, puncture-proof sole. Trapped between the hard place of earth-burying embarrassment and soul-destroying heartbreak caused only by the power of love. Of lust. Of immediate need and desire.

She watches her walk away, wiping her beer-covered hand on the back of her jeans. Her eyes drift from her hand to her jeans. To her legs. Her thighs. Her…

"Oi! Love! Pint please, yeah?"

A voice, deeper than the one she wanted to hear, breaks her train of thought. Of look. She raises her head and looks at his face: his cheeks flushed with alcohol, the red hints on his nose and forehead telling her he'd probably had enough already.

"Oi! D'you hear me?"

Her face hardens. She'd heard him. A little too loudly for her liking.

"Certainly, sir," she replies, politeness getting the better of them both. Reaching down to the shelf below she selects a glass without looking. One eye she keeps on him, the other follows the girl with the sea green eyes. He turns to look at what she sees. He notices the tight jeans. The legs. The thighs. The…

"Fuck me! She's got an arse on her!"

His bluntness surprises her. Offends her. Impresses her. She couldn't help but laugh as she pulled his pint.

"You really have a way with words, mate!", her voice tumbling out of her mouth with her laughter. He grins, a knee-jerk reaction, taken aback by the sudden merriment and mirth.

"No, really, love. Look at it! You have got to be blind not to see that that is some arse right there!"

She splutters the price of the pint out as she puts the glass down in front of him and then starts to laugh some more. A richer laugh this time. Genuine. Relaxed.

"Admit it, love," as he hands over the exact change, "you were checking her out more than I was and I definitely would!"

A belly laugh. Full. Deep. Embodies. Embraces her entirely. His face alight with pleasure and surprise, he winked at her and moved back to his group. His friends. His stags.

Subconsciously she looks over. She looks around. Looks. For her. Her eyes search for the sea-green.

They discover a mess.

The bar—her bar—a sea of empties, crumpled crisp packets and pools of sticky, unwanted, uninvited drink splattered over the tables, floor, bar.

She pauses. The search for the sea-green forgotten. Abandoned in favour of the bigger picture. Relinquished for reputation. Put aside for her profession. A sacrifice so often made. Her heart put on the shelf to let her strive for success. A lifelong dream. A want that became a dream. Her mind shifts. Drifts. Back to the first time. That fleeting glance. That chance meeting as a child with the building that soon became a love. Her love. Her passion. Her reason for sacrifice. One love surrendered for another. Bricks and mortar instead of hugs and hands. Cellars and kitchens replacing kisses and cuddles. Barrels and bottles before romance and desire. This bar. This building. This dream. This is what filled her life. Brought her peace. Kept her safe. The roaring fire in the corner of the snug, echoed in her home above, kept her warm on those cold winter eves. Customers had become regulars and then became locals. Became friends. Some felt like family. A few felt like home.

She strolls between the optics and pumps, collecting a cloth as she goes. Gently she takes hold of the waist of this evening's work colleague. He stands up straighter and steps in to let her pass. He smiles cheekily.

"Well, I never knew I was your type, dear." She shakes her head and taps his bum in reply.

"Keep on dreaming, sweet cheeks. It's never gonna happen." An old routine, repeated every time. It had started long ago. Before this bar. Before her love had become her own to cherish. He had followed her from place to place. From job to job. Wanting nothing more than what he had. Nothing more than the security she gave him. Nothing more than the friendship they had created. The family they had developed. She adored him. He was good to her. Kept her smiling when times were tricky. He was good for her. Didn't let her become too obsessed. Too distracted by her dream to overlook life. To forget to have fun. He was her friend. Her closest friend. Her family.

She reaches the sink and turns on the tap, rinsing and wringing the cloth till the water runs clear. She picks up a second, dry, cloth and bundles it into her back pocket. Then picks up a spray bottle and tucked the trigger into her belt. She's armed and ready to return the bar to its glory. To its beauty before they had come in. Before the customers. Before opening. He always ridiculed her for her habit to keep the bar spotless. Always wanting every customer to walk in and see the building how she saw it. To appreciate the love within the walls. The love that kept the building warm and smiley.

"It's like trying to work with Kim and bleeding Aggie with you! Just collect the empties and wipe the tables. You should be charming the money out of their pockets, not plumping the cushions under their backsides." She could feel those words from him as she started. But she could not help it. Could not stop herself from tirelessly cleaning the bar. Keeping it looking how she sees it. The image in her mind pushing to become a reality. She starts on the bar. Her solid oak bar. Not varnished, but waxed to protect the grain. A more tactile experience. Marked with rings from glasses and spilt drinks, she mops up the wet, sprays and polishes with the dry. Moving down the bar, pushing in front of the regulars. Her locals. Her friends. Some see her coming and step back, out of her way, before she reaches them. Two-thirds of the way along she reaches the remainder of an accidental wave. A visible memory of the destruction of satin over sand. She catches her breath. Her hand unwilling to erase the memory. The moment. The powerful, world stopping, love. She places the cloth next to the reminder. Turns her head. Her eyes start their search again. Her hands work automatically as her mind remembers. Dry cloth and spray-gun join the abandoned wet cloth on the bar. Her feet turn to join the eyes on the search. She mindlessly collects empties, stacking pint glasses, as she moves. Checking each table, each group, each pair. Tidying as she moves. Looking to find her. The girl with the sea-green eyes, who made her dream of satin over sand. Who stopped the world with the lightest of touches. Who could not be found; could not be seen amongst the crowd of nameless people.

Her shoulders sag at the thought of losing her. At the thought of breaking the connection on an accidental wave. A moment stretched too long. Too far. Over-stretched to breaking point. The stack of glasses teeters, reaching from waist to shoulder, balancing in the crook of her arm. She supports the stack and weaves her way back to the bar. Back behind the bar. Back to safety. He takes the stack from her, smiling gently at her as he separates the glasses. He had seen the moment. Observed the satin over sand. Caught his own breath with the destruction of the accidental wave. He hadn't seen her respond to someone like that. Had never seen her world stop by the look in another's eyes. Not once. Not even when this bar, this building, this dream became hers to love. To cherish. Not even when her eyes sparkled and glittered with emotion the day she first opened the doors. The day she allowed the world to see her dream. To share her love.

She heads back out into the jollity of the crowds. Moves to the back of the room and turns into the snug. She falters as she looks in. Frozen in the archway. The girl with the sea-green eyes, at the far table. In the corner. Next to the fire.

She holds her breath. Her heart pounding in her chest. No longer dragging at the floor. A rush of blood to her face. She hesitates, then steps in through the archway. Steps in towards the girl with the sea-green eyes. Desperate to speak. To touch. For satin over sand. Her mind races. Searched frantically for the right words. The smooth words. The words that will impress. Mentally she stumbles, her world moving in and out of soft focus. Her breathing quickens. Shallow. Desirable? Her feet move too quickly. Too eager to make contact. Too willing to look into the sea-green. She reaches the table before her mind makes the decision. Before the words form complete in her brain. She stands there. At the table. In front of the girl. She can feel the world slowing. Blurring. Halting. Those sea-green eyes look up at her. Questioningly. An expectant smile forms at her lips. Tearing herself away from the sea-green. Wanting to rectify her reputation. She opens her mouth and prays the words are ready. Only to hear her voice speak.

"You, er, you finished with these?"

She closes her eyes, stunned by the words her brain chose to utter. Her head drops. She picks up the empty glasses and turns away.

"Way to go, loser."

A SIMPLE GESTURE

by

Effi Mai

Effi Mai has wanted to be a writer since her mother started making up stories for her to calm her temper as a child. She lives in civilization with her cat Crayon but originally she's from a small village in Wales surrounded by sheep and farmer's sons. She writes theblog Fisforr.com that mentions unicorns far too much and is hoping to get her novels published in the distant, rainbow future.

I stretched out my hand, our knuckles just grazing. I felt happy.

Bee's hair was tied up with a handkerchief today. A few strands had fallen out, but the ringlets looked so pretty. She had leant into me just before we'd left the house and it smelt of oranges. Her skin always smelt of talcum powder from her late-night bath and was soft to touch. She always covered herself in the stuff, whereas I hated the feel of it on my hands.

A nice walk to end with a picnic on the bench was planned. A most relaxing day. The bench overlooked the White Swan bar, where we'd first met up and shared our most intimate moments. Or where it used to be. Now, just a site of pulled apart stones, scattered bricks and powdered memories.

We had left the house separately. It was the silliest thing we did, since we met just at the end of our road, and yet it was a routine. If we had just been friends we probably wouldn't have thought twice about leaving together, arms linked. Yet we were so careful. Too careful, most of the time.

"Lordy, imagine seeing you here." Bee jumped as the shadow of the man covered us. She got up, quickly smoothing down her beige trousers and giving her brother a kiss on the cheek.

"Yes, nice to see you," she replied. I couldn't see her face, but I knew she wasn't genuinely smiling.

"Having a little catch-up over lunch?" He noted the crumbs of cheese and the nub of bread laid out on paper between us. He pointedly ignored me. "Ladies sure know how to have the idle life, I do say!"

I gritted my teeth.

Bee hadn't got home until nearly midnight just last night. It used to worry me when she was so late, imagining her lying somewhere under the remains of some building. But I had got used to it over the past year. I would wait for her in our room doing meaningless tasks like folding the laundry or wiping down already clean surfaces. When she finally came in, she would always be clutching the tin hat to her chest, and then would set it down, making sure the W was facing the wall.

She only told me a little of what she saw. Instead she told me snippets of information that she heard in conversation. Did you know that dipping a piece of thread in oil makes for a much easier darn? Or that Henry the Eighth wrote "Greensleeves" for his mistress? He had her beheaded two years after marrying her. She would rest her head on my lap after she'd washed the dirt from herself and her wet hair would tickle my thighs.

The horrible stories, the things no person should ever see, were etched across her face during the day, and then plagued her dreams at night. I often woke up to her screaming and tearing at the sheets, pushing me away as I tried to comfort her.

I looked back up from the bench.

"You know, trying to get out in this charming weather." Bee gestured to the clear sky, and cleared her throat. I felt rather uncomfortable sitting down while both of them were standing, but I also felt very conscious of how my creased linen dress might appear to a man who always looked like he'd stepped straight out of the Times.

"Did you get Mother's invite then? She's got a chap for you to meet: he works at my firm, jolly good company."

My heart lurched. Not that you could tell from the stony expression I had kept since her brother had arrived and ruined our picnic. We should have stayed in the flat and had our food in bed.

Our bed was the best part of our flat. It was cast iron with beautiful detail in the headboard. To visitors of course it was Bee's bed. My room was just down the narrow hallway, but I knew that if they looked closely they would be able to tell that the single mattress had never been slept on, and my thumbed books, thick candles and jewellery box were all on Bee's second dressing table.

Bee glanced at me quickly and then shook her head.

"People are talking," I heard him mutter, before he turned and walked away.

Bee sat back down. She put her hand next to mine and pressed her little finger into me. It was a simple gesture but it made me feel safe.

*

"Here," Bee smiled, handing me a glass of water.

"Because this is really going to make me much less nervous, I must say."

She stopped rooting around in her pockets and turned to me, her face inches from mine. She still made my heart beat faster and breath quicken. All the things I'd read about in books that Father brought home for me. She terrified me.

She was more tanned than I remembered from two weeks back, more freckles too; her hair cut shorter now, but the curls still twisted up, prettily falling around her neck.

"What reason did you give him?"

"John?"

Bee touched my arm. Fleeting as it was, it still distracted me from what she said. I looked at the hand, wanting to reach out and touch it. Still not daring.

"We don't have to talk about him," I said, cutting across her, and then apologising for doing so. "And you don't have to keep saying sorry all the time."

"Sorry," Bee grinned. I pressed my tongue against the inside of my cheek. She laughed.

"Would you rather a proper drink? There's a new sort of ale, quite marvellous."

I shook my head and allowed myself to lean against her as she looked around the room, her cheeks pink.

"Shall we sit?"

"I like it here."

From where we stood, with Bee's arm on the end of the small bar, we could talk amongst ourselves in the corner without anyone spotting us right away and coming up to bother us. Just last week someone Bee had been friendly with before had come up to greet us warmly. It was nice to feel welcome but I hated the knowing looks and the cheeky winks.

"Why are we being like this?"

I frowned and pulled away slightly, my blouse catching on the big metal buttons of her coat.

"Like what?"

"Different—you might say awkward." I sighed, and she stared hard at me. "Are you regretting meeting me?"

"Of course not!"

"Was it hard to get away from him?"

She referred to John, who I had meant to be meeting, but had cancelled. Again. I, of course, never told my parents of this change of plans. I wouldn't know what to say.

"Then what is it?"

"Nothing."

"Is it John? Do you feel guilty?"

"No, it's not John, I don't want him, I don't want to be with him."

"Then what?"

"I'm scared."

"Scared?"

"Yes—I'm not you, this is all new." She took a sip of her water and slammed the glass down on the little table next to us. The barmaid looked up momentarily and then went back to listening to her wireless.

"Have I ruined it? Is it because I kissed you?"

The words hung in the air. I gulped. Glancing quickly behind me to see the usual crowd of women dancing, I reached out and cupped her cheek. Her eyes widened as I put my lips to hers, pressing my red ones against her pink ones hard and shivering as her hand cupped my waist and her fingers grazed against the thin fabric of my skirt.

I breathed out and kept my face close to hers and whispered.

"I'm scared because I so want to be alone with you."

Bee tucked a piece of hair back behind my ear and then kissed it. I felt her tongue and her hot breath and suddenly, for the first time, I didn't care about anyone else but us. Just as if it was us in the world. She shrugged my coat over my shoulders and buttoned the top two up, her fingers lingering before she clasped my hands in her own.

"Let me take you home."

*

"Anne? I'm over here!" I weaved my way through the bar, tugging down the hem of my dress. Bee hugged me warmly. "It's lovely to see you again."

I nodded and slid into the bench opposite her. She was already sipping on a thick beer.

"Am I late?"

"Of course not! I'm early. I've got the night off. It's such a pleasure knowing that work isn't looming. It's like a black cloud hanging over me all day even when the sun is shining! Did you know that three black clouds clumped together means there is an argument about to happen? '

"You work as a warden?"

"Yes, just started full time."

"Do you like it?"

Bee looked down at the frothy glass and took a long sip. She tapped her short nails against it and took a deep breath. My stomach twisted at the awkward silence and the fear that she might get up and leave.

"Let's not talk about work things, shall we? Have you been doing anything fun?"

"I'm afraid not," I replied.

"John not been taking you anywhere? That is preposterous!"

I bit at my nail. John's name had come up ever so quickly.

"No, he's busy, you know."

"Being a conscientious objector?"

I was about to object myself but then found myself nodding.

"He got the feathers in the post yesterday, no name," I said quietly.

"There's never a name."

I looked at my surroundings. The tavern was a small room but it was packed full of people. The women were dressed like men in their wide trousers and buttoned up shirts.

"They're the *lumberjills*," Bee said.

"The what?"

"The women who go out to work in the country—that sort of thing."

"Oh, right."

"You look worried," she told me. I realised I had been avoiding looking at her. I was nervous. Nervous of being so close to her, nervous that it was just the two of us.

"I've never been here."

"It's not the done thing." I smoothed my hair down. The curls had stayed in place after I'd almost scorched my scalp with the hot rollers. "You look very pretty."

"I thought women weren't actually allowed. And thank you."

Bee laughed out loud and I blushed furiously. She pushed her drink towards me.

"It's a different sort of bar. I will treat you but try it first." I lifted the heavy, glass worried that it would mess up my lipstick. "Go on! It's tasty."

Just as I was bringing it to my lips, she held her hands over mine to make me drink. I swallowed a big mouthful. It tasted bitter and cold and delicious. Her hands stayed over mine until I'd pushed the glass back.

"I'll get you one." She pulled herself up. "Try and relax, Annie."

I couldn't help but let my face split into a smile. She was the only one that called me that.

Some couples were dancing in the corner, kicking out and spinning around. I wondered what it would feel like to dance with Bee. Would it be different with a woman? I imagined Bee putting her hands around my waist and in my hair. Would she kiss me? I shivered.

She made me jump as she slammed two more drinks down on the sticky table. She sat down next to me this time, her thigh inches from mine. I felt hot and clasped the drink in appreciation.

"We could go dancing?" she said. "If you would like to."

The beer mat clung to her drink as she sipped, the name of the pub—"The White Swan"—blazed over it.

I looked at Bee. Her short hair curled at her cheeks and her collar looked stiff and handsome. She had little make-up on from what I could see. She was beautiful.

"I'd like us to stay here, if that's alright." I leaned on the bench and swung my legs under the table.

"Sounds perfect."

Bee stretched and then put her hand on top of mine. And it stayed like that as we drank and chatted the night away.

*

He was cross with me. For trying to get out of meeting his family. I could tell just by the way he slammed on the breaks of the motor and it shuddered to a holt. We were outside his parents' house. A first for me.

I pulled my plum cardigan around my shoulders and scrunched my hands on my lap, waiting for him to speak.

"Don't say anything unwise." He got out, slamming the door and not bothering to open mine like he promised. I struggled with the handle then kicked it hard with my shoe. I noticed the brown leather was scuffed once we stood by the front door. John rolled his eyes.

"Pinch your cheeks."

"Pinch what?"

"Pinch your cheeks: you're looking so pale you look unwell." He cupped my face and then pulled the skin between his thumb and forefinger. The door opened and a small framed woman stood in a black dress.

"Oh my boy, you're getting taller all the time."

John pulled me closer to greet her.

"Mother, I haven't grown in ten years." He took my arm. "This is Anne."

I could sense the woman looking me up and down but kept the smile on my face.

"Hullo."

"Well yes. Lovely to meet you Anne. Come in."

She said my name in an odd way. Like not even the name had met her expectations.

The front room of their home was almost as big as my entire house. I could hear my father's voice in my head telling me what a waste of space it all was. The clock ticked loudly. I felt dizzy.

"Where is Elizabeth?" John demanded to know as we sat down.

"Upstairs, changing from that ghastly uniform."

"I can hardly believe you let her move out," he continued, shrugging off his long coat. "I mean, really, Mother."

She poured out the tea. The china was so thin it looked like it would break just by picking it up.

"Well never mind now, tell us about your job."

I couldn't listen again to the description of what John did. I could almost tell people off by heart now from the times I had heard his little speech about the bank. I sighed and John glared at me.

I heard a door open behind me and John spun around frowning.

"Where have you been? We've been here fifteen minutes just." The tall woman sat down opposite and tucked her bare feet under a cushion.

"I'm here now."

"This is Anne. Anne, this is Elizabeth, my sister." She leaned across and shook my hand. Her hands were soft, like freshly washed bed clothes.

"We're both named after queens then, although I must say Queen Elizabeth was a bit of a better queen than any Queen Anne. No Elizabeths were beheaded."

"Elizabeth, how rude! What are you doing saying things like that?"

"Yes, be quiet," John agreed. I caught his sister's eye and quickly looked away inwardly smiling. A queen's name. The thought made me feel warm inside and I chided myself for being so silly.

"Dinner will be ready soon. John, join me in the dining room a minute?" His mother nodded at me and turned on her heel with her son following.

"Smile, it may never happen."

"What won't?" I asked Elizabeth, confused.

"Do you know that you should always crack eggs at both ends? Lets the devil out. I always do it. I get plenty of them from the Rayburn Farm. Got my contacts, you know."

I nodded in case what she had said was a question. Elizabeth got off the couch and proffered her hand to pull me up. It was a simple gesture but it made me feel more welcome in the house. We stood face to face: I could see the birthmark on her neck, her skin tightening as she breathed in. I felt myself going red.

"You and I are going to get on just fine." She clasped both of my hands in hers. "And you should call me Bee."

More Titles from Freya Publications

SunKissed

An original anthology of Lesbian Love Stories by some of the UK's best indie writers.

The Mask of the Highwaywoman by Niamh Murphy

Evelyn Thackeray, the spirited daughter of a wealthy aristocrat, is en route to meet her future husband when a gang of vicious outlaws attacks her stagecoach. In spite of Evelyn's terror, she is intrigued by the leader of the gang, a beautiful Highwaywoman called Bess. Increasingly entranced by Bess and the prospect of adventure, Evelyn puts up little resistance when she is kidnapped. However, she begins to suspect there is a lot more to her captor than she initially thought and what started as a light-hearted escapade rapidly turns into a desperate escape and a frantic struggle for survival.

Niamh Murphy's debut novel is not just a swashbuckling lesbian romance, but also a gripping tale of love and betrayal.

Strains from an Aeolian Harp
by Emma Rose Millar

1922: Charlie is a chancer, with a taste for gin, ragtime and women. Underneath his veneer of assurance however, is a man with a terrible burden of guilt. Fuelled by his fatal addiction to opium, Charlie's violent temper soon inflicts devastating consequences on the three women who love him, dragging each of them into a world they could never have imagined. Strains from an Aeolian Harp is the story of one woman's enduring strength and of the fragile bond between women in a society filled with prejudice and misogyny.

Loving Amélie
by Sasha Faulks

Chris Skinner is struggling to recover from a lost love affair: an experience that has altered him. Previously happy enough to labour alongside his older brother Peter in their family restaurant, he briefly found new perspective on life and love in the form of the inimitable French beauty, Amélie Bénoit, who happened into his bistro one day and later into his bed.

Amélie is passionate and artistic, if fickle and flawed in her own appealing way. They shared a love of real food and great sex. Then she left him.

Entrusted with the care of their baby daughter, Amélie Christina, Chris embarks on a journey that takes him from London to Paris, via his childhood in the Midlands, to make sense of the ties that bind him: family unity, friendships and obsessive love.

The Garrow Boy

by Sasha Faulks

"She needs to see them for what they are. I love her, and I want her to love me. I would have my own child. Why can't you just help me?"

When recently widowed Jess Martin leaves London for a new life in the country, she swaps the constraints of her well-meaning in-laws for the mixed morality of small-town rural England. Together with her young daughter, who has been deaf from birth, she sets about renovating a cottage for their future, unaware that they will both find love and liberation in a surprising place...

Jess is befriended by good-time-girl Suzy Fallon and finds herself falling prey to the charms of local widower Nigel Gilbert, whose parents are the hub of the small village's social scene.

In the meantime she appears to have secured the attention, and affection, of the Garrow boy, the son of an elderly villager who has a reputation for witchcraft. Unwilling to give in to the small-mindedness and gossip-mongering of her superficially God-fearing neighbours, Jess can't help feeling there is more to Lee Garrow's story than meets the eye... although she hopes he won't distract her from making the most of her new life, and her new romance.

A tale of Heathcliff and Cathy for our time.

Crossing the Line
by Toni James

Rachel Ryder is training for the British Mountain Championships. After years of hard work, she's in the best shape of her life and a favourite to win the Championship. So the last thing she needs is a broken arm and a distracting encounter with a beautiful doctor. Matters become even more confusing when Rachel's treacherous ex-girlfriend arrives on the scene, determined to stop at nothing to win her back.

With the championships approaching and her heart in a storm, Rachel is forced to choose between the woman she lost, the woman she has found and her opportunity to realise the ambition of a lifetime.

The Lost Resort
by Toni James

When Eve Harper finds her lover in the arms of another woman, she's forced to face up to some uncomfortable truths; she's single, the wrong side of forty and she's running out of wine! There's nothing else for it but to sell everything and take an extended holiday in Greece. With her unruly younger sister in tow, Eve embarks on a tumultuous journey of self-discovery, and en route she meets Annie, a troubled teacher from England, Heidi, an ambitious hotelier, and JJ, a cute bartender with an uncanny gift for cocktails. When she arrives at The Lost Resort, a women-only hotel on the Greek Island of Lesbos, Eve finds her own slice of paradise and, with temperatures rising and passion in the air; she wonders where it will all end. But this is only the beginning. The Lost Resort is the first in a series of funny, romantic novels set on the Greek island of Lesbos. It is a story about friendship, family and the restorative power of love.

For more information or to purchase any of our titles please visit www.freyapublications.com or www.amazon.co.uk.